KS3

ENGLISH
PRACTICE TEST PAPERS

PAUL BURNS

Contents

ACKNOWLEDGEMENTS

The author and publisher are grateful to the copyright holders for permission to use quoted materials and images.

P46-47 Extract © Telegraph Media Group Limited 2011

All images are © Shutterstock.com

Every effort has been made to trace copyright holders and obtain their permission for the use of copyright material. The author and publisher will gladly receive information enabling them to rectify any error or omission in subsequent editions. All facts are correct at time of going to press.

Published by Letts Educational

An imprint of HarperCollins*Publishers* Ltd
1 London Bridge Street
London SE1 9GF

9780008299163

First published 2014

This edition published 2018

10 9 8 7 6 5 4 3 2 1

© HarperCollins*Publishers* Limited

British Library Cataloguing in Publication Data.

A CIP record of this book is available from the British Library.

Commissioning Editor: Rebecca Skinner
Author: Paul Burns
Project Managers: Shelley Teasdale and Belinda Jones
Editorial: Michael Groom
Cover Design: Amparo Barrera
Inside Concept Design: Letts Educational
Text Design and Layout: Aptara®, Inc.
Artwork: Letts Educational and Aptara®, Inc.
Production: Natalia Rebow
Printed by Martins the Printers, Berwick upon Tweed

Introduction

How to Use the Practice Test Papers

About these Practice Test Papers

At the end of Key Stage 3, tests will be used by your teachers to determine your level of achievement in English.

In this book, you have three sets of test papers (A, B and C) that will allow you to track your progress in Key Stage 3 English. They will help you to identify your strengths and weaknesses in the subject and prepare you for the tests and assessments at the end of Key Stage 3.

The test papers will:
*   test your knowledge and understanding of reading, writing and comprehension
*   provide practice on how to answer questions on these topics by helping to familiarise you with the different question styles that appear in test papers
*   enable you to mark your work and score your performance
*   record results to track progress
*   help you to move confidently on to your GCSE course.

How to Use the Test Papers

*   The questions in these test papers have been written in the style that you will see in actual tests.
*   While you should try to complete the different sections in each set in the same week, you should complete sets 1, 2 and 3 **at intervals** through Key Stage 3, or Year 9.
*   Make sure you leave a reasonable amount of time between each assessment – it is unrealistic to expect to see much improvement in just a few weeks. Spreading out the sets will mean you have an opportunity to develop and practise any areas you need to focus on. You will feel much more motivated if you wait for a while, because your progress will be much more obvious.
*   If you want to re-use the papers, write in pencil and then rub out the answers. However, don't repeat the set too soon or you will remember the answers and the results won't be a true reflection of your abilities.

Each set of papers (A, B and C) provides one complete assessment. Each set includes:
1. a reading test paper, including reading material on which the questions are based (1 hour 15 minutes)
2. a writing test paper, which consists of a longer writing task and a shorter writing task (1 hour 15 minutes)
3. three Shakespeare test papers: one on *Romeo and Juliet;* one on *As You Like It*; and one on *Macbeth*, including extracts from the scenes on which the questions are based (45 minutes).

Sets
ABC

KEY STAGE 3

Introduction

English

Introduction

How to Prepare for the Tests

Revision:
After covering the necessary topics, read through your notes from school or course notes. Perhaps use a revision guide to recap the key points. You could also add notes and diagrams to a mind map.

Equipment you will need:
- pen(s), pencil and rubber
- ruler
- a watch or clock to time yourself.

When you feel that you're properly prepared, take the first set of test papers.

Taking the Tests

1. Remember, each set of tests is made up of **three** test papers. The following table will give you the time you should spend on each, and the marks they are worth:

Paper	Reading test paper	Shakespeare test paper	Writing test paper
Time	75 mins	45 mins	75 mins
Marks	32	18	50 (20/30)

2. Choose a time to take the first paper when you can work through it in one go. Make sure you have an appropriate place to sit and take the test, where you will be uninterrupted.
3. Answer **all** the questions in the test. If you are stuck on one question, move on and come back to it later. Tests often start with easier questions. These become more complex, and cover more than one topic, as you work through the test papers.
4. Read the questions **carefully**, so that you understand exactly what you need to do. Don't spend too long on any one question.
5. The number of marks allocated to each question is shown. This will tell you how many key points are needed in the answer.
6. Stay calm! Don't be fazed by questions. Read the question carefully and think it through.

Approaching the Reading Test

The reading tests can be quite intimidating when you first see them. Each of them comes with five pages of reading material, on three topics. Don't worry. The reading material can easily be read in the 15 minutes allowed, and there is plenty of time to answer all the questions. Here are some tips to help you to do your best:

1. Use the whole of the 15 minutes allocated to read through the reading material. In a real exam, you will not be allowed to open your question and answer booklet until the 15 minutes are up. While you are reading, you might find it helpful to underline or highlight parts that you find interesting.
2. Remember that you can and **should** refer back to the reading material once the 15 minutes are up.
3. Timing is key. There are three sections, each containing questions on one of the texts. Therefore, you should try to spend no more than 20 minutes on each section. It is not uncommon for students to do well on the first few questions but fail to complete the paper, and end up with low marks as a result.

4. Within each section, note how many marks are awarded for each answer. Some questions might give you only one mark, while others can gain you five. The number of marks is usually reflected in the amount of space you are given for the answer.

During the Test

To do well in any test or exam you need to understand what each question requires you to do. In these papers, the questions test a variety of skills that you use when reading. You need to know what the 'instruction' words in the questions mean so you can show that you possess these skills. Here are some words and phrases that the questions might use, with a brief explanation of what they mean:

1. **Pick out a phrase/phrases or word/words:** Take the words directly from the text. A phrase is a group of words.
2. **Support with a quotation:** Again, use exact words from the text, and use quotation marks.
3. **Identify:** Give an example or quotation.
4. **Evidence from the text:** This can be a quotation or it can be put in your own words – a quotation is usually safer.
5. **Explain:** Don't just repeat what's already there – make it clearer, showing that you understand what it means.
6. **Give reasons:** Support your point by referring back to the text, either using quotations or your own words.
7. **What is the effect of/explain the effect:** What is the effect on you, the reader? How does it make you feel, for example? What does it make you think about?
8. **How does the writer…?** This will be about how the writer uses language. Think about the choice of words, how different words or phrases might affect you, and how the text is set out.
9. **Fill in the box or complete a chart:** Make sure you know exactly what you are required to do and you put your answers in the correct spaces.
   Five-mark questions usually have bullet points underneath. These are there to help you and you cannot get good marks if you do not cover all the points. It is a good idea to write a paragraph on each bullet point and support each with at least one quotation from the text and a comment on each quotation.

Approaching the Shakespeare Test

Which Papers Should You Do?

- Each set of practice test papers in this book includes three Shakespeare papers: one on *Romeo and Juliet*; one on *As You Like It*; and one on *Macbeth*.
- While there are three plays in the set, only do the **one you have studied at school**. There will be two scenes from it to read, and one question on them.
- It is possible that you go to a school where the teachers are teaching a different Shakespeare play. If you are in this position, it will still be helpful to look at the questions in this book to give you an idea of the type of question you can expect. You might even be able to make up your own question, in a similar style, for the play you have studied. When you take the test for real, you will be asked about the play you have studied!
  Similarly, you may have studied one of the three plays used here but have focused on particular scenes which are different from those used in these practice papers. It will still be useful to have a go at the tests in this book, but you may also want to try out the questions using the scenes you have concentrated on in class, rather than the extracts printed here.

- Make sure you know the play you have studied. If you have not yet covered it when you want to start doing practice tests, you should leave the Shakespeare test and come back to it when feel you have enough knowledge to have a go.

During the Test

1. Read the question carefully, making sure you understand what you need to do. It may focus on language, character, themes or performance. Underline or highlight key points.
2. Skim-read the extracts you have been given and make notes on the page, underlining or highlighting useful quotations.
3. Plan your answer. Do not take too long doing this and do it in whatever way suits you best. Your plan is not marked.
4. Make sure you **use a quotation to support every point you make**. Remember PEE: Point, Evidence, Explanation.
5. Write about both of the extracts, paying special attention to any differences between them.
6. Write in paragraphs, in good, clear English.
7. When you have finished, read through your work to make sure that you have included everything you wanted to.

Approaching the Writing Test

This test assesses your ability to adapt your writing to different forms, purposes and audiences, as well as testing the accuracy of your spelling, grammar and punctuation.

People often find it difficult to revise for writing tests. There are two main things you can do:

1. Revise what is required for different audiences, purposes and forms. You might be asked to write in order to:
   - explain or describe something
   - argue a point of view or persuade someone to your point of view
   - give advice
   - entertain your readers, by using your imagination.

   Or you could be asked to write in different forms, for example:
   - a letter
   - a story
   - a diary
   - a leaflet.

   Sometimes the question will specify an audience, for example:
   - teenagers
   - children
   - adults – such as parents, teachers or a head teacher.

   All these things affect the organisation and the style of your writing. Make sure you know what the expected layout of each form looks like, and use it.

2. Look carefully over the written work you have done in the past and make a list of errors you tend to make in spelling, punctuation and grammar. Then work hard at putting them right.

There are two tasks on each paper and you should make sure you allocate your time properly, spending more time on the longer task than on the shorter task.

The two tasks will be very different from each other. For example, one might be in the form of a letter and the other in the form of a short story. One might be about trying to argue a point, while the other might ask you to explain something.

Remember that your marks are not based on how much you write. **Aim for quality, not quantity.**

During the Test

1. Read the question carefully, making sure you understand what you are being asked to do:
   - What is its purpose?
   - Who is the intended audience?
   - What form should it be in?
2. Quickly plan your answer. For the longer task, you might be provided with a planning frame but you can plan in whatever way suits you best.
3. Make sure you write in paragraphs and try to connect them with appropriate words and phrases.
4. Pay close attention to correct spelling, punctuation and grammar.
5. When you have finished, check your work carefully and correct any errors that you spot.

How to Use the Answers and Mark Scheme

When you've sat the test, you, or a parent or guardian, should use the mark scheme to mark it. You could mark the test together. It's often helpful for you to discuss the answers with someone as you go through the mark scheme.

You should:
- read the suggested answers and marks given in the section at the back of this book
- look at your own answers and decide what mark you deserve for each one
- add up the marks to give you your overall score out of 100
- keep your mark for next time, so that you can compare how you do after each set.

Tips for the Top

After sitting a test paper:
1. Try to analyse your performance. For questions that only gained a low mark, identify where you went wrong. Are there gaps in your knowledge and understanding? Were there areas where you were under-prepared?
2. Go back through your test papers and make a note of all the questions where you lost marks and the reasons for losing them.
3. Use study guides and workbooks at home to reinforce your learning and develop your skills.
4. Undertake another set after a reasonable amount of time has passed. Go back to your last practice set and compare your results to see how far you have progressed and what you may still need to concentrate on.

Set

A

KEY STAGE 3

Reading Test
Paper

English

Into the Woods!

Reading Test Paper

Into the Woods!

First name   _____

Last name   _____

Date   _____

Instructions

- Before you start to write, you have 15 minutes to read the reading material (pages 9–14). There are three texts. Make sure you read all three.

- During this time you should not look at the questions on the following pages.

- You then have **1 hour** to answer all the questions on pages 15–21.

- Answer all the questions.

- Write your answers in the spaces provided.

- When you have finished, check your work carefully.

After you have completed the test, you can mark your answers using pages 107–110 of the Answers and Mark Scheme section of this book.

Enter the marks for each answer in the small box next to your answer.

At the bottom of each page put the total marks for that page.

Enter your marks in the boxes below and add them up to get your total out of 32.

Page	15	16	17	18	19	20	21	Total mark	Maximum mark
Score									32

Reading Material

Contents

People have always been fascinated by woods and forests. In old stories and tales they are places of mystery, creating fear and excitement. Some people still find them scary places.

Others see them as places of adventure, where you can go on long walks and enjoy nature, or take part in activities like canoeing and abseiling.

In these texts we see what going into the woods means to different people (or animals), and how it makes them feel.

"The Way Through the Woods"

In this poem, Rudyard Kipling describes a place where a road used to run through some woods. The road was closed many years ago and has now disappeared altogether under trees and undergrowth . . .

They shut the way through the woods
Seventy years ago.
Weather and rain have undone it again,
And now you would never know
5 There was once a road through the woods
Before they planted the trees.
It is underneath the coppice[1] and heath
And the thin anemones.
Only the keeper[2] sees
10 That, where the ring-dove broods,
And the badgers roll at ease,
There was once a road through the woods.

Yet, if you enter the woods
Of a summer evening late,
15 When the night-air cools on the trout-ringed pools
Where the otter whistles his mate,
(They fear not men in the woods,
Because they see so few)
You will hear the beat of a horse's feet,
20 And the swish of a skirt in the dew,
Steadily cantering[3] through
The misty solitudes,
As though they perfectly knew
The old lost road through the woods . . .
25 But there is no road through the woods.

Rudyard Kipling

---

[1]*Coppice – an area of undergrowth and small trees*
[2]*Keeper – the gamekeeper, whose job it is to look after and control birds and animals for a landowner*
[3]*Cantering – (a horse) going at a medium pace, between a trot and a gallop*

Home　　**Gallery**　　**About Us**　　**Contact Us**

WESTERLY WOODS ADVENTURE PARK: a world of adventure waiting for you!

Fun and adventure on your doorstep

Wondering what to do in the school holidays? Fancy a few days away not too far from home? Or would you just like a day out with family or friends? Here at Westerly Woods we've got something for everyone.

The woods themselves are beautiful all the year round: when the first flowers are appearing in spring; in the full glory of summer; when the leaves turn red and gold in the autumn; and even when the ground is covered in a blanket of snow. Whatever the time of year, you're welcome to enjoy Nature's bounty at Westerly.

Walks in the woods

There are miles of well-maintained footpaths through the woods. They're all well sign-posted and you're welcome to set off on your own. However, if you prefer company and the guidance of an expert, you can book one of our guided walks.

Our well-trained and experience Woodland Rangers offer a wide variety of walks, for all levels of experience. You can book them as an individual or as a group of any size. Click here for more details.

Adventure trails

If you're looking for a bit more of an adrenaline buzz, you might want to have a go at one of the Westerly Adventure Trails.

If you're one of life's thrill-seekers, you'll love our trails! These are walks through the woods with a difference. Around every corner there's a new challenge – swinging on ropes, battling through swamps or hurtling down slides. All this and more is waiting for you at Westerly Woods.

Whether you're young or old, with your family or a group of friends, we can organise an adventure to suit you. Scouts and Guides, school and youth groups, work colleagues – even stag and hen parties – can be catered for at Westerly. Find out more by clicking here!

Stay a while

Sometimes a day out just isn't enough – especially when there's as much to see and do as there is at Westerly Woods. So why not stay a while? Spend the night, the weekend or even longer. Make yourself at home.

Try one of our log cabins

Here at Westerly we've built a whole village of rustic log cabins, clustered around the tranquil natural lake that lies at the centre of the woods. They can sleep anything from two to eight people, are built from traditional materials and finished to the highest standards. Inside you'll find every modern convenience to make your stay comfortable and stress-free. Get in touch here for details of prices and availability.

Or what about a camping barn?

For bigger groups we've got two specially designed camping barns. A bit less sophisticated than our cabins, these are designed to take large parties. Basic cooking and bathroom facilities are provided, but everything else you bring yourselves. It's just like camping but without a tent!

These barns make superb venues for corporate adventure weekends as well as being ideal for groups of young people. Click here for details.

Education through fun

For school and youth groups, we can provide tailor-made educational activities. Young people learn just from being here, and we aim to help them develop physical and mental skills through fun. But we also have a team of well-qualified and enthusiastic Woodland Rangers. They not only instruct and supervise young people on the adventure trails, but also have a wealth of knowledge about nature and the environment to share with them. For details of educational activities and resources, click here.

So what are you waiting for? Get in touch today and we'll guarantee you the adventure of a lifetime!

"The Wild Wood"

"The Wild Wood" from *The Wind in the Willows* by Kenneth Grahame

The Wind in the Willows *describes the adventures of a group of animals that live on the banks of a river, near the Wild Wood. One afternoon, Mole, who has never been into the Wild Wood before, leaves his friend Ratty's house to explore the woods, ignoring Ratty's warnings . . .*

It was a cold still afternoon with a hard steely sky overhead, when he slipped out of the warm parlour into the open air [. . .] and with great cheerfulness of spirit he pushed on towards the Wild Wood, which lay before him low and threatening, like a black reef in some still southern sea.

There was nothing to alarm him at first entry. Twigs crackled under his feet, logs tripped him, funguses on stumps resembled caricatures, and startled him for the moment by their likeness to something familiar and far away; but that was all fun, and exciting. It led him on, and he penetrated to where the light was less, and trees crouched nearer and nearer, and holes made ugly mouths at him on either side.

Everything was very still now. The dusk advanced on him steadily, rapidly, gathering in behind and before; and the light seemed to be draining away like flood-water.

Then the faces began.

It was over his shoulder, and indistinctly, that he first thought he saw a face: a little evil wedge-shaped face, looking at him from a hole. When he turned and confronted it, the thing had vanished.

He quickened his pace, telling himself cheerfully not to begin imagining things, or there would be simply no end to it. He passed another hole, and another, and another; and then – yes! – no! – yes! Certainly a little narrow face, with hard eyes, had flashed up for an instant from a hole, and was gone. He hesitated – braced himself up for an effort and strode on. Then suddenly, and as if it had been so all the time, every hole, far and near, and there were hundreds of them, seemed to possess its face, coming and going rapidly, all fixing on him evil glances of malice and hatred: all hard-eyed and evil and sharp.

If he could only get away from the holes in the banks, he thought, there would be no more faces. He swung off the path and plunged into the untrodden places of the wood.

Then the whistling began.

Very faint and shrill it was, and far behind him, when first he heard it; but somehow it made him hurry forward. Then, still very faint and shrill, it sounded far ahead of him, and made him hesitate and want to go back. As he halted in indecision it broke out on either side, and seemed to be caught up and passed on throughout the whole length of the wood to its furthest limit. They were up and alert and ready, evidently, whoever they were! And he – he was alone, and unarmed, and far from help; and the night was closing in.

Then the pattering began.

He thought it was only falling leaves at first, so slight and delicate was the sound of it. Then as it grew it took a regular rhythm, and he knew it for nothing else but the pat-pat-pat of little feet, still a very long way off. Was it in front or behind? It seemed to be first one, then another, then both. It grew and it multiplied, till from every quarter as he listened anxiously, leaning this way and that, it seemed to be closing in on him. As he stood still to hearken,[1] a rabbit came running hard towards him through the trees. He waited, expecting it to slacken pace, or to swerve from him into a different course. Instead the animal almost brushed him as it dashed past, his eyes staring. 'Get out of this, you fool, get out!' the mole heard him mutter as he swung round a stump and disappeared down a friendly burrow.

---

[1]*Hearken – listen*

Questions 1–5 are about "The Way Through the Woods" by Rudyard Kipling (on page 10 of the reading material).

1. The way through the woods has disappeared, partly because of nature and partly because of people.

    Give two ways in which people are responsible.

    _____

    _____

    1 mark

2. In the first stanza (lines 1–12), the poet gives examples of animals and plants that live in the woods. From the first stanza pick out examples of:

    (a) a flower _____

    (b) a bird _____

    (c) a mammal _____

    1 mark

3. The phrase 'only the keeper sees' (line 9) suggests the keeper is different from other people. How do you think he is different?

    _____

    _____

    _____

    _____

    2 marks

4. The second stanza of the poem ends with an ellipsis (…) before the final line. What effect does this have?

    _____

    _____

    _____

    _____

    1 mark

SUBTOTAL

5. How does the poet use language to give an impression of mystery and the supernatural?

You should comment on:

- words and phrases he uses to describe the wood in the first stanza
- what he says you will hear in the woods
- the effect his language has on the reader.

_____

_____

_____

_____

_____

_____

_____

_____

_____

_____

_____

Questions 6–10 are about Westerly Woods Adventure Park (pages 11–12 of the reading material).

6. How does the writer describe the woods in winter?

_____

1 mark

7. According to the section headed "Walks in the woods", why might some people prefer to go on a guided walk rather than setting off on their own? Give two reasons.

_____

_____

_____

1 mark

8. Look at the section headed "Try one of our log cabins". In the chart below are descriptions of people who might be attracted to the log cabins. In column 2 write down a phrase from the paragraph that would appeal to these people. The first one is done for you.

2 marks

People being appealed to	Phrase from the text
People who like their 'home comforts'	_Every modern convenience_
People who feel they need a good rest	
People who like to meet new people on holiday	
People who like to feel they're close to nature	

SUBTOTAL

9. Explain why the camping barns at Westerly Woods might appeal to large groups of young people.

_____

_____

_____

_____

10. Look again at the section headed "Adventure trails". How does the writer use language to make the trails sound exciting and fun?

Refer to specific words and phrases from the section and comment on them.

_____

_____

_____

_____

_____

_____

_____

_____

11. Write down a phrase from the first paragraph which shows that Mole is happy and optimistic.

1 mark

_____

12. Pick out two phrases from the second paragraph which 'personify' the woods, giving the impression that the woods are alive.

1 mark

_____

_____

13. What do the following quotations tell us about Mole's attitude to the faces in the woods? Complete the following table. The first one has been done for you.

2 marks

He quickened his pace, telling himself not to begin imagining things . . .	_Mole thinks that the 'faces' are not real and that, if he is confident, they will go away._
And then – yes! – no! – yes!	
Certainly a little narrow face, with hard eyes, had flashed up	
. . . all fixing on him with evil glances of malice and hatred	

SUBTOTAL

14. Read the last paragraph again.

(a) The first sentence states: 'He thought it was only falling leaves at first'. How does the writer imply that the sound is **not** that of falling leaves?

_____

_____

(b) What might the reader expect to be making the noise before Mole sees the rabbit?

_____

_____

15. Which of the following statements about the text are true and which are false? Write 'True' or 'False' in the box. The first one has been done for you.

Mole knows the Wild Wood very well.	False
Mole imagines the faces.	
The faces and noises are all made by the rabbit.	
At the end of the extract we do not know whose faces they are.	
At the end of the extract Mole is safe.	
At the end of the extract the rabbit is safe.	

16. How does the author, Kenneth Grahame, create an atmosphere of fear and tension in "The Wild Wood"?

5 marks

Think about:
- Mole's feelings when he sets off on his walk
- the things that happen that worry him
- how Mole's feelings change from the beginning to the end of the extract
- the language used to describe the woods and Mole's feelings.

_____

_____

_____

_____

_____

_____

_____

_____

_____

_____

_____

_____

_____

_____

SUBTOTAL

Set

A

KEY STAGE 3

Shakespeare
Test Paper

English

*Romeo and Juliet, As
You Like It and Macbeth*

Shakespeare Test Paper

Romeo and Juliet, As You Like It and *Macbeth*

First name _____

Last name _____

Date _____

Instructions

In the following pages you will find three questions which assess your reading and understanding of Shakespeare. Each is on a different play:

Romeo and Juliet	page 23
As You Like It	page 28
Macbeth	page 33

- **Only** answer the question on the play you have studied.

- Read the question carefully.

- Write your answer on lined paper.

- You have **45 minutes** to complete the task.

- When you have completed the test, you can mark your answer using pages 115–118 of the Answers and Mark Scheme section of this book.

- Enter your mark below:

MAXIMUM MARK	18		ACTUAL MARK	

Romeo and Juliet

Romeo and Juliet

Act 3, Scene 2, lines 1–71
Act 3, Scene 5, lines 1–59

In the first extract, after their secret marriage, Juliet is waiting for her nurse to bring her news about Romeo. In the second, she is saying goodbye to Romeo after their first night together.

What impressions might an audience get of Juliet and her feelings for Romeo from the way she speaks and acts in these extracts?

Support your ideas by referring to both of the extracts which are printed on the following pages.

Please note that line numbers may not be the same as those in the edition you used in class.

Romeo and Juliet

Act 3, Scene 2, lines 1–71

In this extract, after Friar Lawrence has married them, Juliet is waiting for Romeo.

JULIET   Gallop apace, you fiery-footed steeds,
Towards Phoebus' lodging. Such a wagoner
As Phaeton would whip you to the west
And bring in cloudy night immediately.
Spread thy close curtain, love-performing night,   5
That runaways' eyes may wink, and Romeo
Leap to these arms, untalked of and unseen.
Lovers can see to do their amorous rites
By their own beauties; or, if love be blind,
It best agrees with night. Come, civil night,   10
Thou sober-suited matron, all in black,
And learn me how to lose a winning match
Played for a pair of stainless maidenhoods.
Hood my unmanned blood bating in my cheeks,   15
With thy black mantle, till strange love grow bold,
Think true love acted simple modesty.
Come night, come Romeo, come thou day in night,
For thou wilt lie upon the wings of night
Whiter than new snow upon a raven's back.   20
Come gentle night, come loving, black-browed night,
Give me my Romeo; and when he shall die
Take him and cut him out in little stars,
And he will make the face of heaven so fine
That all the world will be in love with night,   25
And pay no worship to the garish sun.
O, I have bought the mansion of a love
But not possessed it, and though I am sold,
Not yet enjoyed. So tedious is this day
As is the night before some festival   30
To an impatient child that has new robes
And may not wear them. O, here comes my Nurse
And she brings news, and every tongue that speaks
But Romeo's name speaks heavenly eloquence.

Enter NURSE *with cords*

How, Nurse, what news? What hast thou there? The cords
That Romeo bid thee fetch?

NURSE   Ay, ay, the cords.   35

JULIET	Ay me! What news? Why dost thou wring thy hands?
NURSE	Ah, well-a-day! He's dead, he's dead, he's dead!
	We are undone, lady, we are undone!
	Alack the day! He's gone, he's kill'd, he's dead!
JULIET	Can heaven be so envious?
NURSE	Romeo can,
	Though heaven cannot. O Romeo, Romeo,
	Whoever would have thought it? Romeo!
JULIET	What devil art thou that dost torment me thus?
	This torture should be roar'd in dismal hell.
	Hath Romeo slain himself? Say thou but 'Ay',
	And that bare vowel 'I' shall poison more
	Than the death-darting eye of cockatrice:
	I am not I, if there be such an 'Ay',
	Or those eyes shut, that makes thee answer 'Ay'.
	If he be slain, say 'Ay'; or if not, 'No':
	Brief sounds determine of my weal or woe.
NURSE	I saw the wound, I saw it with mine eyes –
	God save the mark – here on his manly breast.
	A piteous corse, a bloody piteous corse;
	Pale, pale as ashes, all bedaub'd in blood –
	All in gore-blood. I swounded at the sight.
JULIET	O break, my heart! Poor bankrupt, break at once!
	To prison, eyes, ne'er look on liberty!
	Vile earth, to earth resign. End motion here;
	And thou and Romeo press one heavy bier!
NURSE	O Tybalt, Tybalt, the best friend I had.
	O courteous Tybalt! Honest gentleman!
	That ever I should live to see thee dead!
JULIET	What storm is this that blows so contrary?
	Is Romeo slaughter'd and is Tybalt dead?
	My dear-loved cousin and my dearer lord?
	Then, dreadful trumpet sound the general doom!
	For who is living, if these two are gone?
NURSE	Tybalt is gone and Romeo banished;
	Romeo that kill'd him, he is banished.

40

45

50

55

60

65

70

Act 3, Scene 5, lines 1–59

In this extract, Romeo is leaving Juliet after they have spent their first night together.

JULIET   Wilt thou be gone? It is not yet near day.
It was the nightingale and not the lark
That pierced the fearful hollow of thine ear.
Nightly she sings on yon pomegranate tree.
Believe me, love, it was the nightingale.   5

ROMEO   It was the lark, the herald of the morn,
No nightingale. Look, love, what envious streaks
Do lace the severing clouds in yonder east.
Night's candles are burnt out, and jocund day
Stands tiptoe on the misty mountain tops.   10
I must be gone and live, or stay and die.

JULIET   Yon light is not daylight, I know it, I.
It is some meteor that the sun exhales
To be to thee this night a torchbearer,
And light thee on thy way to Mantua.   15
Therefore stay yet: thou need'st not be gone.

ROMEO   Let me be ta'en. Let me be put to death.
I am content, so thou wilt have it so.
I'll say yon grey is not the morning's eye,
'Tis but the pale reflex of Cynthia's brow.   20
Nor that is not the lark whose notes do beat
The vaulty heaven so high above our heads.
I have more care to stay than will to go.
Come death, and welcome. Juliet wills it so.
How is't, my soul? Let's talk. It is not day.   25

JULIET   It is, it is. Hie hence! Be gone, away!
It is the lark that sings so out of tune,
Straining harsh discords and unpleasing sharps.
Some say the lark makes sweet diversion.
This doth not so, for she divideth us.   30
Some say the lark and loathed toad change eyes.
O, now I would they had changed voices too,
Since arm from arm that voice doth us affray,
Hunting thee hence with hunt's-up to the day.
O, now be gone; more light and light it grows.   35

ROMEO   More light and light: more dark and dark our woes

NURSE	Madam.	
JULIET	Nurse?	
NURSE	Your lady mother is coming to your chamber.	
	The day is broke; be wary, look about.	40

Exit

JULIET   Then, window, let day in and let life out.

ROMEO   Farewell, farewell. One kiss and I'll descend.

They kiss; ROMEO *descends*

JULIET   Art thou gone so? Love, lord, ay husband, friend,
I must hear from thee every day in the hour,
For in a minute there are many days.   45
O, by this count I shall be much in years
Ere I again behold my Romeo.

ROMEO   Farewell.
I will omit no opportunity
That may convey my greetings, love, to thee.   50

JULIET   O think'st thou we shall ever meet again?

ROMEO   I doubt it not, and all these woes shall serve
For sweet discorses in our times to come.

JULIET   O God, I have an ill-divining soul!
Methinks I see thee, now thou art so low,   55
As one dead in the bottom of a tomb.
Either my eyesight fails, or thou look'st pale.

ROMEO   And trust me, love, in my eye so do you.
Dry sorrow drinks our blood. Adieu, adieu.

Exit

As You Like It

What do these scenes tell us about the themes of family love and loyalty in the play?

Support your ideas by referring to both of the extracts printed on the following pages.

As You Like It

Act 1, Scene 1, lines 1–79

In this extract (which opens the play), Orlando confronts his older brother, Oliver, about the way he has treated him since their father's death.

Enter ORLANDO *and* ADAM

ORLANDO   As I remember, Adam, it was upon this fashion
bequeathed me by will but poor a thousand crowns,
and, as thou sayest, charged my brother, on his
blessing, to breed me well: and there begins my
sadness. My brother Jaques he keeps at school, and   5
report speaks goldenly of his profit. For my part,
he keeps me rustically at home, or, to speak more
properly, stays me here at home unkept. For call you
that keeping for a gentleman of my birth, that
differs not from the stalling of an ox? His horses   10
are bred better; for, besides that they are fair
with their feeding, they are taught their manage,
and to that end riders dearly hired. But I, his
brother, gain nothing under him but growth; for the
which his animals on his dunghills are as much   15
bound to him as I. Besides this nothing that he so
plentifully gives me, the something that nature gave
me his countenance seems to take from me. He lets
me feed with his hinds, bars me the place of a
brother, and, as much as in him lies, mines my   20
gentility with my education. This is it, Adam, that
grieves me; and the spirit of my father, which I
think is within me, begins to mutiny against this
servitude. I will no longer endure it, though yet I
know no wise remedy how to avoid it.   25

ADAM   Yonder comes my master, your brother.

ORLANDO   Go apart, Adam, and thou shalt hear how he will
shake me up.

Enter OLIVER

OLIVER   Now, sir! What make you here?

ORLANDO   Nothing. I am not taught to make anything.   30

OLIVER   What mar you then, sir?

ORLANDO	Marry, sir, I am helping you to mar that which God made, a poor unworthy brother of yours, with idleness.	
OLIVER	Marry, sir, be better employed, and be naught awhile.	
ORLANDO	Shall I keep your hogs and eat husks with them? What prodigal portion have I spent, that I should come to such penury?	35
OLIVER	Know you where you are, sir?	
ORLANDO	O, sir, very well; here in your orchard.	
OLIVER	Know you before whom, sir?	40
ORLANDO	Ay, better than him I am before knows me. I know you are my eldest brother; and, in the gentle condition of blood, you should so know me. The courtesy of nations allows you my better, in that you are the first-born; but the same tradition takes not away my blood, were there twenty brothers betwixt us. I have as much of my father in me as you; albeit, I confess, your coming before me is nearer to his reverence.	45
OLIVER	What, boy! (*strikes him*)	50
ORLANDO	Come, come, elder brother, you are too young in this. (*seizes him*)	
OLIVER	Wilt thou lay hands on me, villain?	
ORLANDO	I am no villain. I am the youngest son of Sir Rowland de Boys. He was my father, and he is thrice a villain that says such a father begot villains. Wert thou not my brother, I would not take this hand from thy throat till this other had pulled out thy tongue for saying so. Thou hast railed on thyself.	55
ADAM	Sweet masters, be patient. For your father's remembrance, be at accord.	60
OLIVER	Let me go, I say.	
ORLANDO	I will not, till I please. You shall hear me. My father charged you in his will to give me good education. You have trained me like a peasant, obscuring and hiding from me all gentleman-like	65

qualities. The spirit of my father grows strong in me, and I will no longer endure it. Therefore allow me such exercises as may become a gentleman, or give me the poor allottery my father left me by testament; with that I will go buy my fortunes. 70

OLIVER   And what wilt thou do? Beg, when that is spent? Well, sir, get you in. I will not long be troubled with you. You shall have some part of your will. I pray you, leave me.

ORLANDO   I will no further offend you than becomes me for my good. 75

OLIVER   Get you with him, you old dog.

ADAM   Is 'old dog' my reward? Most true, I have lost my teeth in your service. God be with my old master! He would not have spoke such a word.

Exeunt ORLANDO *and* ADAM

Act 2, Scene 3, lines 30–77

In this extract, Adam has just warned Orlando not to return home because of the danger he is in from his brother.

ORLANDO   Why, whither, Adam, wouldst thou have me go? 30

ADAM   No matter whither, so you come not here.

ORLANDO   What? Wouldst thou have me go and beg my food?
Or with a base and boisterous sword enforce
A thievish living on the common road?
This I must do, or know not what to do. 35
Yet this I will not do, do how I can.
I rather will subject me to the malice
Of a diverted blood and bloody brother.

ADAM   But do not so. I have five hundred crowns,
The thrifty hire I saved under your father, 40
Which I did store to be my foster-nurse
When service should in my old limbs lie lame
And unregarded age in corners thrown.
Take that, and He that doth the ravens feed,
Yea, providently caters for the sparrow, 45
Be comfort to my age! Here is the gold.
And all this I give you. Let me be your servant.
Though I look old, yet I am strong and lusty;
For in my youth I never did apply

Act 5, Scene 5, lines 1–50

In this extract, Macbeth is preparing to fight the armies of Malcolm and Macduff.

*Enter MACBETH, SEYTON and
soldiers, with drum and colours*

MACBETH Hang out our banners on the outward walls;
The cry is still, 'They come'. Our castle's strength
Will laugh a siege to scorn; here let them lie
Till famine and the ague eat them up.
Were they not forced with those that should be ours,   5
We might as well have met them dareful, beard to beard,
And beat them backward home.

A cry within of women

What is that noise?

SEYTON It is the cry of women, my good lord.

MACBETH I have almost forgot the taste of fears;
The time has been, my senses would have cooled   10
To hear a night shriek and my fell of hair
Would at a dismal treatise rouse and stir
As life were in't. I have supped full with horrors;
Direness familiar to my slaughterous thoughts
Cannot once start me. Wherefore was that cry?   15

SEYTON The queen, my lord, is dead.

MACBETH She should have died hereafter.
There would have been a time for such a word.
Tomorrow, and tomorrow, and tomorrow
Creeps in this petty pace from day to day
To the last syllable of recorded time;   20
And all our yesterdays have lighted fools
The way to dusty death. Out, out, brief candle!
Life's but a walking shadow, a poor player
That struts and frets his hour upon the stage
And then is heard no more. It is a tale   25
Told by an idiot, full of sound and fury
Signifying nothing.

Enter a MESSENGER

Thou com'st to use thy tongue.
Thy story quickly.

MESSENGER	Gracious my lord,
	I should report that which I say I saw,
	But know not how to do't.

| MACBETH | Well, say, sir. | 30 |

MESSENGER	As I did stand my watch upon the hill
	I looked toward Birnam and anon methought
	The wood began to move.

| MACBETH | Liar and slave! |

MESSENGER	Let me endure your wrath if't be not so;
	Within this three mile may you see it coming.	35
	I say, a moving grove.

MACBETH	If thou speak'st false,
	Upon the next tree shall thou hang alive
	Till famine cling thee; if thy speech be sooth,
	I care not if thou dost for me as much.
	I pull in resolution and begin	40
	To doubt th'equivocation of the fiend
	That lies like truth. 'Fear not, till Birnam Wood
	Do come to Dunsinane', and now a wood
	Comes toward Dunsinane. Arm, arm, and out!
	If this which he avouches does appear,	45
	There is no flying hence nor tarrying here.
	I 'gin to be aweary of the sun
	And wish th'estate o'th'world were now undone.
	Ring the alarum-bell! Blow wind, come wrack;
	At least we'll die with harness on our back.	50

Set
A

KEY STAGE 3

Writing Test
Paper

English

Happy Acres

Writing Test Paper

Happy Acres

First name _____

Last name _____

Date _____

Instructions

- There are two writing tasks in this paper.

- The test is **1 hour and 15 minutes** long.

- You should spend: **45 minutes** on Section A (the longer writing task)
  30 minutes on Section B (the shorter writing task).

- You may spend the first 15 minutes planning your answer to Section A. Your plan will not be marked.

- Section A has 30 marks.

- Section B has 20 marks.

- Write your answer on lined paper.

- When you have finished, check your work carefully.

When you have completed the test, you can mark your answer using pages 123–128 of the Answers and Mark Scheme section of this book.

- Enter your marks below:

	Mark	Maximum mark
Section A		30
Section B		20
Total		50

Section A

Longer Writing Task

A Weekend at Happy Acres

You are a journalist working for a magazine aimed at people with families. Recently you received the following note from your manager:

> I would like you to spend the weekend, with your family, at the Happy Acres Holiday Park so that you can review it for our readers.
>
> All expenses are paid but this is not an advertisement. I want an honest account of your experience. Please include:
> - some factual information about the park
> - the positive aspects of your experience
> - the negative aspects of your experience
> - your judgement on whether this is a good place to spend a weekend with your family.

Write your report on your visit to Happy Acres.

Section B

Shorter Writing Task

Summer Job at Happy Acres

The Happy Acres Holiday Park has placed an advertisement in the local paper. This is the advertisement:

Outgoing, enthusiastic people wanted!

To meet increased demand during the summer holidays, Happy Acres Holiday Park is looking for temporary staff to work with children.

The job involves supervising children from 4 to 14 while they enjoy our facilities, organising games and creative play, and dealing with any situation that might arise!

Successful candidates will be:
- reliable
- enthusiastic
- creative
- patient
- flexible.

If you think you've got the right qualities and experience, please apply in writing to Ms A Caffley, Happy Acres Holiday Park, Springwood, Westby.

Write a letter applying for the job.

Reading Test Paper

Set
B

Catching the Train

English

First name _____

Last name _____

Date _____

Instructions

- Before you start to write, you have **15 minutes** to read the reading material (pages 42–47). There are three texts. Make sure you read all three.

- During this time you should not look at the questions on the following pages.

- You then have **1 hour** to answer all the questions on pages 48–54.

- Answer all the questions.

- Write your answers in the spaces provided.

- When you have finished, check your work carefully.

After you have completed the test, you can mark your answers using pages 110–112 of the Answers and Mark Scheme section of this book.

- Enter the marks for each answer in the small box next to your answer.

- At the bottom of each page put the total marks for that page.

- Enter your marks in the boxes below and add them up to get your total out of 32.

Page	48	49	50	51	52	53	54	Total mark	Maximum mark
Score									32

Catching the Train

Reading Material

Contents

Since Victorian times, trains and railways have been an important part of people's lives.

For some, they are just a way of getting from one place to another – sometimes quickly and efficiently, and sometimes not!

For others – whether they collect toy trains, 'spot' trains or like to takes trips and holidays to exotic places – they are a source of endless fascination and enjoyment.

In this page, from a website designed for school pupils, the writer explains how and why the railways grew in Victorian Britain, and how their growth changed people's lives. The Great Exhibition of 1851 was a huge exhibition of products from all over the world and attracted thousands of visitors.

The Railways of Victorian Britain

Most of the working people who came to the Great Exhibition arrived by rail, often from the north of England. King's Cross Station was opened in 1850 and there were nearly 7,000 miles of track linking London with the towns of the Midlands and the North.

Source 1: Great Exhibition, 1851

The most popular way of getting to the Great Exhibition was by buying a ticket that included a return rail journey and entry. These could cost 4, 5 or 6 shillings. Hundreds of thousands of people took advantage of these day trips, which were the idea of Thomas Cook.

He booked trains from all over Britain to take people to the Great Exhibition and charged them a fixed price for the return trip and the entry ticket. Overnight he had invented the 'day out'.

Source 2: Beach, Eastbourne

As Cook's business grew, he began to offer excursions to more and more places, including trips to other European countries. Soon the railway companies began to run their own excursions.

At first, railway companies tried to avoid dealing with the masses and preferred to run trains that only offered second- and first-class carriages. They also tried to avoid stopping their trains at every station. But in 1844 the Railways Act stated that at least one train a day must stop at every station, and include third-class carriages. Now large numbers of Victorians could afford to travel.

Source 3: Fun-fair

The railways were to make a huge difference to the leisure activities of the Victorians. Not only were opportunities for holidays and day trips increased, but sporting events also grew in popularity. Special trains and trips were run to take people to the races, cricket matches or the FA Cup Final, which was held for the first time in 1872. It was not only spectators that benefited: the football clubs that were being started in many of Britain's cities could now travel away to play against each other.

In 1888 the Football League was founded. It was made up of professional teams. It would have been impossible for the first teams to travel to play away matches without regular trains. So the railways were very important in the development of professional football in Britain.

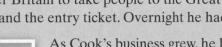

Source 4: Cocoa advert

But many of these developments only affected the better-off people in Britain. For most working people, the important changes were the cheap day returns that many railway companies started to offer.

In 1871 bank holidays were introduced and so began the great British tradition of the day at the seaside, along with sticks of rock, candy-floss, walks along the pier, fun-fair rides and fish and chips. The first fish and chip shops appeared in the 1860s.

Source 5: Victorian country railway station

"Saviours of the Train"

from *The Railway Children* by E. Nesbit

Peter; his older sister, Bobbie; and his younger sister, Phyllis, live near a busy railway line. In this chapter they have gone to pick cherries near the line when they notice something strange and possibly very dangerous . . .

They were almost at the gate when Bobbie said: 'Hush. Stop! What's that?'

'That' was a very odd noise indeed – a soft noise, but quite plainly to be heard through the sound of the wind in the tree branches, and the hum and whir of the telegraph wires. It was a sort of rustling, whispering sound. As they listened it stopped, and then it began again.

And this time it did not stop, but it grew louder and more rustling and rumbling.

'Look,' cried Peter suddenly, 'the tree over there!'

The tree he pointed at was one of those that have rough grey leaves and white flowers. The berries, when they come, are bright scarlet, but if you pick them, they disappoint you by turning black before you get them home. And, as Peter pointed, the tree was moving – not just the way trees ought to move when the wind blows through them, but all in one piece, as though it were a live creature and were walking down the side of the cutting.

'It's moving!' cried Bobbie. 'Oh, look! And so are the others. It's like the woods in *Macbeth*.'

'It's magic,' said Phyllis, breathlessly. 'I always knew the railway was enchanted.'

It really did seem a little like magic. For all the trees for about twenty yards of the opposite bank seemed to be slowly walking down towards the railway line, the tree with the grey leaves bringing up the rear like some old shepherd driving a flock of green sheep.

'What is it? Oh, what is it?' said Phyllis. 'It's much too magic for me. I don't like it. Let's go home.'

But Bobbie and Peter clung fast to the rail and watched breathlessly. And Phyllis made no movement towards going home by herself.

The trees moved on and on. Some stones and loose earth fell down and rattled on the railway metals far below.

'It's *all* coming down,' Peter tried to say, but he found there was hardly any voice to say it with. And, indeed, just as he spoke, the great rock, on the top of which the walking trees were, leaned slowly forward. The trees, ceasing to walk, stood still and shivered. Leaning with the rock, they seemed to hesitate a moment, and then rock and trees and grasses and bushes, with a rushing sound, slipped right away from the face of the cutting and fell on the line with a blundering crash that could have been heard half a mile off. And a cloud of dust rose up.

'Oh,' said Peter, in awestruck tones, 'isn't it exactly like when the coals come in? If there wasn't any roof to the cellar and you could see down.'

'Look what a great mound it's made!' said Bobbie.

'Yes, it's right across the down line,' said Phyllis.

'That'll take some sweeping up,' said Bobbie.

'Yes,' said Peter, slowly: he was still leaning on the fence. 'Yes,' he said again, still more slowly.

Then he stood upright.

'The 11.29 down hasn't gone by yet. We must let them know at the station, or there'll be a most frightful accident.'

'Let's run,' said Bobbie, and began.

But Peter cried, 'Come back!' and looked at Mother's watch. He was very prompt and businesslike, and his face looked whiter than they had ever seen it.

'No time,' he said, 'it's two miles away, and it's past eleven.'

'Couldn't we,' suggested Phyllis breathlessly, 'couldn't we climb up a telegraph post and do something to the wires?'

'We don't know how,' said Peter.

'They do it in war,' said Phyllis, 'I know I've heard of it.'

'They only cut them, silly,' said Peter, 'and that doesn't do any good. And we couldn't cut them if we got up, and we couldn't get up. If we had anything red, we could get down on the line and wave it.'

'But the train wouldn't see us till it got round the corner, and then it could see the mound just as well as us,' said Phyllis, 'better, because it's much bigger than us.'

'If we only had something red,' Peter repeated, 'we could go round the corner and wave to the train.'

'We might wave anyway.'

'They'd only think it was just *us*, as usual. We've waved so often before. Anyway, let's get down.'

They got down the steep stairs. Bobbie was pale and shivering. Peter's face looked thinner than usual. Phyllis was red-faced and damp with anxiety.

'Oh, how hot I am!' she said, 'and I thought it was going to be cold. I wish we hadn't put on our –' she stopped short, and then ended in quite a different tone – 'our flannel petticoats.'[1]

Bobbie turned at the bottom of the stairs.

'Oh, yes,' she cried; '*they're* red! Let's take them off.'

---

[1] *Petticoat – a sort of dress or skirt worn as underwear*

"Beijing to Shanghai Railway"
Diary of a 4h 48m Journey

New high-speed rail links are opening all over the world. These extracts are from a diary written by journalist Peter Foster on his journey between China's two biggest cities.

08.30: Our first glimpse into the future comes in the shape of the Beijing South Railway Station, a giant glass dome that's propped up on stilts. It looks like a flying saucer has just landed from outer space.

China has built more than 300 of its super-modern railway stations during the decade-long railway building boom, symbols of its growing power; much as the great London stations like Euston, Paddington and King's Cross were for the Victorians.

08.45: After putting the bags through an airport-style scanner, and submitting to a peremptory waft of a security guard's wand, we reach the 'Boarding Gate' for Train G1 – the 09.00 service to Shanghai.

A barrier opens with a wave of your ticket and the passengers are swept down to the platforms on banks of escalators. The number of each carriage is helpfully displayed on a moving digital display.

08.50: Settle into a First Class seat. The legroom on the plush, crimson corduroy seat is generous, and there's a footrest and plug for the laptop, with an airline-style tray table that folds out from the armrest. It's all neat, but not wildly flashy.

09.00: And we're off, gliding out of Beijing South behind a Chinese-built CRH-380BL locomotive. The platform is so clean I can see the guard's reflection in the polished granite as we pass. Within three minutes we're travelling at 180kmh; after five minutes the electronic speed readout shows 247kmh; and seven minutes after departure we've hit the top operating cruising speed of 300kmh (186mph). At this rate, with a brief stop in Nanjing, we'll reach Shanghai in 4 hours, 48 minutes.

09.30: Even after 30 minutes the sensation of speed is remarkable. It feels like we're in an airliner, blasting down the runway, just moments away from getting airborne. (Obviously hoping that's not the case today.) A hostess sets a refreshing cup of green tea down on my table. Even at this speed, the surface barely ripples.

09.50: Another train comes blasting down the line in the opposite direction. This must be one of the test bunnies. There have been some rumblings recently that China's railways might have been built too fast, cutting corners on safety. Engineers deny this. By the time this line opens on Friday the service will have already have been running flat-out (but empty) for a month, with 1,500 trains clocking up 2 million kilometres of dry runs.

10.30: Go for a stroll up the train and, having been quite pleased to have been allocated a seat in first class, now find myself suffering from serious seat envy issues. First class is not, as I had fondly imagined, the best seat in the house. That title indisputably belongs to the 'executive sight-seeing class' right at the front of the train. There are six flat-bed pods – like an airline business class seat – which look straight out over the driver's head and down the tracks. (Cost £170, one way.)

11.09: Time to test the 'facilities'. Happy to report they are very clean and comfortable, with a full-length dress mirror behind the door. (A major advance on the hole-over-the-tracks toilet I last used on a local train from Chengde to Beijing a few weeks back.) The modern vacuum flush is a little startling, but highly efficient.

11.40: Rural China is flashing by outside the window. We're flying through the countryside at about 40ft (nearly 80 per cent of the track is built on raised concrete pylons) while straw-hatted farmers till fields dotted with the tombs of their ancestors, which they work around like an English farmer might circumvent an old oak tree. Some trudge behind mechanical rotavators, others have mules to plough the land, while the majority hoe manually between their lines of crops. Two hours ago it was fields of maize common to north China, but now the fields have morphed into the rice paddies of the warmer, wetter south . . .

12.00: Lunch time. There is a great deal to praise about this train, but the food isn't among its plus points. The carriage fills with the sickly smell of steamed cabbage as fellow passengers open their VIP lunch trays – steamed rice, bok choi,[1] sweetcorn, a chicken leg and some beef and vegetables. It's the Chinese equivalent of a school dinner.

12.32: Arrive Nanjing. We're on the fast train today, only making one stop to Shanghai. The longer version, taking in all 24 stations on the line, takes five-and-a-half hours.

---

[1] Bok choi – a vegetable, sometimes called 'Chinese cabbage'

Questions 1–5: *The Railways of Victorian Britain* (page 43 of the reading material).

1 mark

1. Give two ways in which the Railways Act made sure more people (especially poorer people) could use the railways.

_____

_____

_____

2 marks

2. How, according to the writer, did Thomas Cook invent the 'day out'?

_____

_____

_____

1 mark

3. The writer mentions a number of important events in the development of the railways. Put the following events in order by putting a number in the box (1–5). The first answer has been done for you.

The Football League was founded	
The Railway Act was passed	1
The first FA Cup Final was held	
Bank holidays were introduced	
King's Cross Station was opened	

4. On either side of the text there are small illustrations, labelled as 'Sources 1–5'. Give **two** reasons why these have been included on the page.

_____

_____

_____

_____

_____

_____

5. How, according to the writer, did the railways have a 'huge' impact on the lives of Victorians?

_____

_____

_____

_____

_____

_____

Questions 6–11 are about "Saviours of the Train" (pages 44–45 of the reading material).

6. What do the children hear that is unusual?

_____

_____

7. Pick out two phrases which make it seem as though the tree is moving deliberately.

_____

_____

_____

_____

8. How does the writer show us that Peter knows a lot about the railway?

_____

_____

_____

_____

_____

_____

9. The children consider several ways of stopping the train. Explain why they decide that each of these would not work:

a) Running to the station to warn the stationmaster.

_____

_____

_____

1 mark

b) Climbing up the telegraph post and 'doing something' to the wires.

_____

_____

_____

1 mark

c) Waving at the train.

_____

_____

_____

1 mark

10. How will the girls' flannel petticoats help them to stop the train?

_____

_____

_____

_____

_____

_____

3 marks

SUBTOTAL

11. What impression do you get of the three 'railway children' from the extract?

Think about:
- how they react when they see the tree and earth moving
- what they do when they realise the train in danger
- how they relate to each other.

Write about all three children.

Use evidence from the text to support your ideas.

_____

_____

_____

_____

_____

_____

_____

_____

_____

_____

_____

_____

_____

12. Write down the phrase from the first diary entry that backs up the writer's statement that the new train represents the future.

1 mark

_____

_____

13. How does the writer show that the platform is very clean?

1 mark

_____

_____

_____

14. What do you infer from the fact that the surface of his tea 'barely ripples'?

1 mark

_____

_____

_____

15. Which of the following aspects make the reader feel that the article has been written during the train journey?

1 mark

Tick two of the statements below. If you tick more than two statements, you will receive no marks.

The article is about a train journey.	
Each section starts with a time.	
The writer describes what he sees.	
There is a lot of information in the article.	
The article is written in the present tense.	

SUBTOTAL

16. How does the writer use his diary to reflect on the contrast between the modern railway and a more traditional way of life?

_____

_____

_____

_____

_____

_____

_____

Shakespeare Test Paper

Romeo and Juliet, As You Like It and *Macbeth*

First name _____

Last name _____

Date _____

Instructions

In the following pages you will find three questions which assess your reading and understanding of Shakespeare. Each is on a different play:

Romeo and Juliet	page 56
As You Like It	page 61
Macbeth	page 66

- **Only** answer the question on the play you have studied.

- Read the question carefully.

- Write your answer on lined paper.

- You have **45 minutes** to complete the task.

- When you have completed the test, you can mark your answer using page 115 and pages 118–120 of the Answers and Mark Scheme section of this book.

- Enter your mark below:

MAXIMUM MARK	18		ACTUAL MARK	

Romeo and Juliet

In these extracts, how does Shakespeare use language to explore ideas about love?

Support your ideas by referring to both of the extracts printed on the following pages.

Romeo and Juliet

Act 1, Scene 1, lines 156–220

In this extract, Benvolio questions his cousin Romeo about his mood and feelings.

ROMEO	Ay me! Sad hours seem long.	
	Was that my father that went hence so fast?	
BENVOLIO	It was. What sadness lengthens Romeo's hours?	
ROMEO	Not having that, which, having, makes them short.	
BENVOLIO	In love?	160
ROMEO	Out.	
BENVOLIO	Of love?	
ROMEO	Out of her favour, where I am in love.	
BENVOLIO	Alas, that love, so gentle in his view,	
	Should be so tyrannous and rough in proof.	165
ROMEO	Alas, that love, whose view is muffled still,	
	Should, without eyes, see pathways to his will!	
	Where shall we dine? O me! What fray was here?	
	Yet tell me not, for I have heard it all.	
	Here's much to do with hate, but more with love.	170
	Why, then, O brawling love, O loving hate,	
	O any thing, of nothing first create!	
	O heavy lightness, serious vanity!	
	Mis-shapen chaos of well-seeming forms!	
	Feather of lead, bright smoke, cold fire, sick health,	175
	Still-waking sleep, that is not what it is!	
	This love feel I that feel no love in this.	
	Dost thou not laugh?	
BENVOLIO	No, coz, I rather weep.	
ROMEO	Good heart, at what?	
BENVOLIO	At thy good heart's oppression.	
ROMEO	Why, such is love's transgression.	180
	Griefs of mine own lie heavy in my breast,	
	Which thou wilt propagate, to have it prest	
	With more of thine: this love that thou hast shown	
	Doth add more grief to too much of mine own.	
	Love is a smoke raised with the fume of sighs;	185

Being purged, a fire sparkling in lovers' eyes;
Being vex'd a sea nourish'd with lovers' tears.
What is it else? A madness most discreet,
A choking gall and a preserving sweet.
Farewell, my coz.

BENVOLIO   Soft! I will go along;   190
And if you leave me so, you do me wrong.

ROMEO   Tut, I have lost myself; I am not here.
This is not Romeo, he's some other where.

BENVOLIO   Tell me in sadness, who is that you love.

ROMEO   What, shall I groan and tell thee?   195

BENVOLIO   Groan? Why, no, but sadly tell me who.

ROMEO   Bid a sick man in sadness make his will:
Ah, word ill urged to one that is so ill!
In sadness, cousin, I do love a woman.

BENVOLIO   I aim'd so near, when I supposed you loved.   200

ROMEO   A right good mark-man! And she's fair I love.

BENVOLIO   A right fair mark, fair coz, is soonest hit.

ROMEO   Well, in that hit you miss: she'll not be hit
With Cupid's arrow; she hath Dian's wit;
And, in strong proof of chastity well arm'd,   205
From love's weak childish bow she lives unharm'd.
She will not stay the siege of loving terms,
Nor bide the encounter of assailing eyes,
Nor ope her lap to saint-seducing gold;
O, she is rich in beauty, only poor,   210
That when she dies with beauty dies her store.

BENVOLIO   Then she hath sworn that she will still live chaste?

ROMEO   She hath, and in that sparing makes huge waste,
For beauty starved with her severity
Cuts beauty off from all posterity.   215
She is too fair, too wise, wisely too fair,
To merit bliss by making me despair:
She hath forsworn to love, and in that vow
Do I live dead that live to tell it now.

BENVOLIO   Be ruled by me, forget to think of her.   220

Act 2, Scene 2, lines 1–69

In this extract from the 'balcony scene', Romeo and Juliet declare their love for each other.

ROMEO   He jests at scars that never felt a wound.

                                     JULIET *appears above at a window*

But, soft, what light through yonder window breaks?
It is the east, and Juliet is the sun.
Arise, fair sun, and kill the envious moon,
Who is already sick and pale with grief,   5
That thou her maid art far more fair than she:
Be not her maid, since she is envious;
Her vestal livery is but sick and green
And none but fools do wear it. Cast it off.
It is my lady, O, it is my love!   10
O that she knew she were!
She speaks yet she says nothing. What of that?
Her eye discourses; I will answer it.
I am too bold. 'Tis not to me she speak.
Two of the fairest stars in all the heaven,   15
Having some business, do entreat her eyes
To twinkle in their spheres till they return.
What if her eyes were there, they in her head?
The brightness of her cheek would shame those stars,
As daylight doth a lamp; her eyes in heaven   20
Would through the airy region stream so bright
That birds would sing and think it were not night.
See, how she leans her cheek upon her hand!
O, that I were a glove upon that hand,
That I might touch that cheek!

JULIET   Ay me!

ROMEO   She speaks.   25
O, speak again, bright angel! for thou art
As glorious to this night, being o'er my head
As is a winged messenger of heaven
Unto the white-upturned wondering eyes
Of mortals that fall back to gaze on him   30
When he bestrides the lazy-pacing clouds
And sails upon the bosom of the air.

JULIET	O Romeo, Romeo! Wherefore art thou Romeo?	
	Deny thy father and refuse thy name.	
	Or, if thou wilt not, be but sworn my love,	35
	And I'll no longer be a Capulet.	

ROMEO	[Aside] Shall I hear more, or shall I speak at this?	

JULIET	'Tis but thy name that is my enemy;	
	Thou art thyself, though not a Montague.	
	What's Montague? It is nor hand, nor foot,	40
	Nor arm, nor face, nor any other part	
	Belonging to a man. O, be some other name!	
	What's in a name? That which we call a rose	
	By any other name would smell as sweet;	
	So Romeo would, were he not Romeo call'd,	45
	Retain that dear perfection which he owes	
	Without that title. Romeo, doff thy name,	
	And for that name which is no part of thee	
	Take all myself.	

ROMEO	I take thee at thy word:	
	Call me but love, and I'll be new baptized.	50
	Henceforth I never will be Romeo.	

JULIET	What man art thou that thus bescreen'd in night	
	So stumblest on my counsel?	

ROMEO	By a name	
	I know not how to tell thee who I am:	
	My name, dear saint, is hateful to myself,	55
	Because it is an enemy to thee.	
	Had I it written, I would tear the word.	

JULIET	My ears have not yet drunk a hundred words	
	Of that tongue's utterance, yet I know the sound:	
	Art thou not Romeo and a Montague?	60

ROMEO	Neither, fair saint, if either thee dislike.	

JULIET	How camest thou hither, tell me, and wherefore?	
	The orchard walls are high and hard to climb,	
	And the place death, considering who thou art,	
	If any of my kinsmen find thee here.	65

ROMEO	With love's light wings did I o'er-perch these walls;	
	For stony limits cannot hold love out,	
	And what love can do that dares love attempt;	
	Therefore thy kinsmen are no let to me.	

As You Like It

What different aspects of love do we see in these extracts?

Support your ideas by referring to both of the extracts printed on the following pages.

As You Like It

Act 1, Scene 2, lines 190–240

In this extract, Rosalind falls in love with Orlando as she watches him wrestling with Charles.

CHARLES	Come, where is this young gallant that is so desirous to lie with his mother earth?	
ORLANDO	Ready, sir; but his will hath in it a more modest working.	
DUKE FREDERICK	You shall try but one fall.	
CHARLES	No, I warrant your grace, you shall not entreat him to a second, that have so mightily persuaded him from a first.	195
ORLANDO	You mean to mock me after, you should not have mocked me before: but come your ways.	
ROSALIND	Now Hercules be thy speed, young man!	
CELIA	I would I were invisible, to catch the strong fellow by the leg.	

They wrestle

ROSALIND	O excellent young man!	200
CELIA	If I had a thunderbolt in mine eye, I can tell who should down.	

Shout. CHARLES *is thrown*

DUKE FREDERICK	No more, no more.	
ORLANDO	Yes, I beseech your grace. I am not yet well breathed.	
DUKE FREDERICK	How dost thou, Charles?	
LE BEAU	He cannot speak, my lord.	205
DUKE FREDERICK	Bear him away. What is thy name, young man?	
ORLANDO	Orlando, my liege, the youngest son of Sir Rowland de Boys.	
DUKE FREDERICK	I would thou hadst been son to some man else: The world esteem'd thy father honourable, But I did find him still mine enemy:	210
	Thou shouldst have better pleased me with this deed, Hadst thou descended from another house.	

But fare thee well; thou art a gallant youth.

I would thou hadst told me of another father.

Exeunt DUKE FREDERICK, *train, and* LE BEAU

CELIA	Were I my father, coz, would I do this?	215
ORLANDO	I am more proud to be Sir Rowland's son,	

His youngest son; and would not change that calling,

To be adopted heir to Frederick.

ROSALIND My father loved Sir Rowland as his soul,

And all the world was of my father's mind.   220

Had I before known this young man his son,

I should have given him tears unto entreaties,

Ere he should thus have ventured.

CELIA   Gentle cousin,

Let us go thank him and encourage him.

My father's rough and envious disposition   225

Sticks me at heart. Sir, you have well deserved.

If you do keep your promises in love

But justly, as you have exceeded all promise,

Your mistress shall be happy.

ROSALIND   Gentleman,

Giving him a chain from her neck

Wear this for me, one out of suits with fortune,   230

That could give more, but that her hand lacks means.

Shall we go, coz?

CELIA   Ay. Fare you well, fair gentleman.

ORLANDO Can I not say, I thank you? My better parts

Are all thrown down, and that which here stands up

Is but a quintain, a mere lifeless block.   235

ROSALIND He calls us back: my pride fell with my fortunes;

I'll ask him what he would. Did you call, sir?

Sir, you have wrestled well and overthrown

More than your enemies.

CELIA   Will you go, coz?

ROSALIND Have with you. Fare you well.   240

Exeunt ROSALIND *and* CELIA

Act 2, Scene 4, lines 1–58

In this extract, Rosalind – disguised as a boy – and Celia and Touchstone arrive in the forest.

Enter ROSALIND, *dressed as a boy,* CELIA, *dressed like a shepherdess, and* TOUCHSTONE

ROSALIND O Jupiter, how weary are my spirits!

TOUCHSTONE I care not for my spirits, if my legs were not weary.

ROSALIND I could find in my heart to disgrace my man's apparel and to cry like a woman; but I must comfort the weaker vessel, as doublet and hose ought to show itself courageous to petticoat. Therefore courage, good Aliena!

CELIA I pray you, bear with me. I cannot go no further.

TOUCHSTONE For my part, I had rather bear with you than bear you; yet I should bear no cross if I did bear you, for I think you have no money in your purse.

ROSALIND Well, this is the Forest of Arden.

TOUCHSTONE Ay, now am I in Arden; the more fool I; when I was at home, I was in a better place: but travellers must be content.

ROSALIND Ay, be so, good Touchstone. Look you, who comes here; a young man and an old in solemn talk.

Enter CORIN *and* SILVIUS

CORIN That is the way to make her scorn you still.

SILVIUS O Corin, that thou knew'st how I do love her!

CORIN I partly guess; for I have loved ere now.

SILVIUS No, Corin, being old, thou canst not guess,
Though in thy youth thou wast as true a lover
As ever sigh'd upon a midnight pillow.
But if thy love were ever like to mine –
As sure I think did never man love so –
How many actions most ridiculous
Hast thou been drawn to by thy fantasy?

CORIN	Into a thousand that I have forgotten.
SILVIUS	O, thou didst then ne'er love so heartily!
	If thou remember'st not the slightest folly
	That ever love did make thee run into,
	Thou hast not loved.
	Or if thou hast not sat as I do now,
	Wearying thy hearer in thy mistress' praise,
	Thou hast not loved.
	Or if thou hast not broke from company
	Abruptly, as my passion now makes me,
	Thou hast not loved.
	O Phoebe, Phoebe, Phoebe!

Exit

ROSALIND	Alas, poor shepherd! Searching of thy wound,
	I have by hard adventure found mine own.
TOUCHSTONE	And I mine. I remember, when I was in love I broke
	my sword upon a stone and bid him take that for
	coming a-night to Jane Smile; and I remember the
	kissing of her batlet and the cow's dugs that her
	pretty chopt hands had milked; and I remember the
	wooing of a peascod instead of her, from whom I took
	two cods and, giving her them again, said with
	weeping tears, 'Wear these for my sake.' We that are
	true lovers run into strange capers; but as all is
	mortal in nature, so is all nature in love mortal in folly.
ROSALIND	Thou speakest wiser than thou art ware of.
TOUCHSTONE	Nay, I shall ne'er be ware of mine own wit till I
	break my shins against it.
ROSALIND	Jove, Jove! This shepherd's passion
	is much upon my fashion.
TOUCHSTONE	And mine; but it grows something stale with me.
CELIA	I pray you, one of you question yond man
	if he for gold will give us any food.
	I faint almost to death.

Line numbers: 30, 35, 40, 45, 50, 55

Macbeth

Macbeth

Act 3, Scene 1, lines 73 to the end
Act 3, Scene 4, lines 83 to the end

In the first extract, Macbeth orders the murder of Banquo and his son, Fleance. In the second, he has just seen Banquo's ghost.

What advice would you give an actor playing Macbeth in these scenes?

Support your ideas by referring to both of the extracts printed on the following pages.

Macbeth

Act 3, Scene 1, lines 73 to the end

In this extract, Macbeth orders the murders of Banquo and his son, Fleance.

MACBETH	Have you consider'd of my speeches? Know
	That it was he in the times past which held you
	So under fortune, which you thought had been 75
	Our innocent self: this I made good to you
	In our last conference, pass'd in probation with you,
	How you were borne in hand, how cross'd, the instruments,
	Who wrought with them, and all things else that might
	To half a soul and to a notion crazed 80
	Say 'Thus did Banquo.'
First Murderer	You made it known to us.
MACBETH	I did so, and went further, which is now
	Our point of second meeting. Do you find
	Your patience so predominant in your nature
	That you can let this go? Are you so gospell'd 85
	To pray for this good man and for his issue,
	Whose heavy hand hath bow'd you to the grave
	And beggar'd yours for ever?
First Murderer	We are men, my liege.
MACBETH	Ay, in the catalogue ye go for men;
	As hounds and greyhounds, mongrels, spaniels, curs, 90
	Shoughs, water-rugs and demi-wolves, are clept
	All by the name of dogs: the valued file
	Distinguishes the swift, the slow, the subtle,
	The housekeeper, the hunter, every one
	According to the gift which bounteous nature 95
	Hath in him closed; whereby he does receive
	Particular addition from the bill
	That writes them all alike: and so of men.
	Now, if you have a station in the file,
	Not i'the worst rank of manhood, say't; 100
	And I will put that business in your bosoms,
	Whose execution takes your enemy off,
	Grapples you to the heart and love of us,
	Who wear our health but sickly in his life,
	Which in his death were perfect.
Second Murderer	I am one, my liege, 105
	Whom the vile blows and buffets of the world
	Have so incensed that I am reckless what
	I do to spite the world.

First Murderer	And I another
	So weary with disasters, tugg'd with fortune,
	That I would set my lie on any chance,	110
	To mend it, or be rid on't.
MACBETH	Both of you
	Know Banquo was your enemy.
Both Murderers	True, my lord.
MACBETH	So is he mine; and in such bloody distance,
	That every minute of his being thrusts
	Against my near'st of life: and though I could	115
	With barefaced power sweep him from my sight
	And bid my will avouch it, yet I must not,
	For certain friends that are both his and mine,
	Whose loves I may not drop, but wail his fall
	Who I myself struck down; and thence it is,	120
	That I to your assistance do make love,
	Masking the business from the common eye
	For sundry weighty reasons.
Second Murderer	We shall, my lord,
	Perform what you command us.
First Murderer	Though our lives—
MACBETH	Your spirits shine through you. Within this hour at most	125
	I will advise you where to plant yourselves;
	Acquaint you with the perfect spy o'the time,
	The moment on't; for't must be done to-night,
	And something from the palace; always thought
	That I require a clearness: and with him –	130
	To leave no rubs nor botches in the work –
	Fleance his son, that keeps him company,
	Whose absence is no less material to me
	Than is his father's, must embrace the fate
	Of that dark hour. Resolve yourselves apart:	135
	I'll come to you anon.
Both Murderers	We are resolved, my lord.
MACBETH	I'll call upon you straight: abide within.

Exeunt Murderers

It is concluded. Banquo, thy soul's flight,
If it find heaven, must find it out to-night.

Exit

Act 3, Scene 4, lines 83 to the end

In this extract, Macbeth has seen the ghost of Banquo at a great feast he is holding after becoming king.

LADY MACBETH	My worthy lord,	
	Your noble friends do lack you.	
MACBETH	I do forget.	
	Do not muse at me, my most worthy friends.	85
	I have a strange infirmity, which is nothing	
	To those that know me. Come, love and health to all;	
	Then I'll sit down. Give me some wine; fill full.	
	I drink to the general joy o' the whole table,	
	And to our dear friend Banquo, whom we miss;	90
	Would he were here! To all, and him, we thirst,	
	And all to all.	
Lords	Our duties, and the pledge.	

Re-enter GHOST OF BANQUO

MACBETH	Avaunt! And quit my sight! Let the earth hide thee!	
	Thy bones are marrowless, thy blood is cold;	
	Thou hast no speculation in those eyes	
	Which thou dost glare with!	
LADY MACBETH	Think of this, good peers,	95
	But as a thing of custom: 'tis no other;	
	Only it spoils the pleasure of the time.	
MACBETH	What man dare, I dare:	
	Approach thou like the rugged Russian bear,	
	The arm'd rhinoceros, or the Hyrcan tiger.	100
	Take any shape but that, and my firm nerves	
	Shall never tremble: or be alive again,	
	And dare me to the desert with thy sword.	
	If trembling I inhabit then, protest me	
	The baby of a girl. Hence, horrible shadow!	105
	Unreal mockery, hence!	

GHOST OF BANQUO *vanishes*

	Why, so: being gone,
	I am a man again. Pray you, sit still.

Set

C

KEY STAGE 3

Reading Test
Paper

English

Young and Old

Reading Test Paper

Young and Old

First name _____

Last name _____

Date _____

Instructions

- Before you start to write you have **15 minutes** to read the reading material (pages 75–80). There are three texts. Make sure you read all three.

- During this time you should not look at the questions on the following pages.

- You will then have **1 hour** to answer all the questions on pages 81–87.

- Answer all the questions.

- Write your answers in the spaces provided.

- When you have finished, check your work carefully.

After you have completed the test, you can mark your answers using pages 113–115 of the Answers and Mark Scheme section of this book.

Enter the marks for each answer in the small box next to your answer.

At the bottom of each page put the total marks for that page.

Enter your marks in the boxes below and add them up to get your total out of 32.

Page	81	82	83	84	85	86	87	Total mark	Maximum mark
Score									32

Reading Material

Contents

When young people meet older people they can have very different reactions. They can gain a lot from the experience, as suggested by our first extract. But sometimes, as when Pip meets Miss Havisham in the second extract, the experience can be disturbing.

When people get older they often look back on their youth. They can be full of regrets and stuck in the past, like Miss Havisham; or, like Thomas Goodman, they can enjoy both their memories and their life today.

"Adopt a Granny" scheme

This article describes a scheme to get young and old people together to make friends and help each other . . .

Traditionally, in Britain and all over the world, grandparents have played a huge role in their grandchildren's lives, looking after them when their parents are busy, playing with them, teaching them useful skills or just lending a sympathetic ear. But recent reports show that more and more children are growing up not knowing their grandparents.

Sometimes, sadly, this is because they have died. More often it is because they simply live too far away. The days of spending your life in the same village or town, living down the street from, or even next door to, members of the extended family, are gone for most of us. Grandparents are more likely to be on the other side of the country or even the other side of the world.

This means grandparents, parents and children are all missing out. We're always hearing about the difficulties young parents have in bringing up their children – perhaps a lot of these problems could be solved by a little bit of timely advice from Nan, Gran or Grandma. Young children, too, miss a lot when they don't get the chance to interact with older people. Grandparents often have more time to play with them and to listen to them, while the benefits of the company of young people for older folk are many. Lots of senior citizens will tell you that being with their grandchildren 'keeps them young'.

That's why we've set up an 'Adopt a Granny' scheme here in Puddington.

The idea is simple. If you're a senior citizen who has something to offer to the young – and perhaps you have no grandchildren of your own – or if you're a parent who thinks your children would benefit from contact with the older generation, get in touch with us now. We'll try to match you up with someone who lives close to you. You can meet, see how you get along – and take it from there!

Stan and Vera have been part of the scheme for two years now and, according to Stan, they've had a 'smashing time' getting to know Alfie and Rhianna, who live just around the corner from them in Bigelow village.

'Our own grandchildren live in Australia,' says Vera. 'We're lucky if we get to see them once a year and Skype just isn't the same. Frankly, we were beginning to find life a bit boring until we joined "Adopt a Granny". It's as if a little bit of sunshine has come into our lives. We always look forward to seeing the children and we feel part of the world again. It's like a new lease of life!'

Of course, there are certain rules we have to keep to for everyone's safety and comfort and certain checks that have to be made. We're a registered charity, working closely with the District Council, and we can assure you that we will make sure everything's properly organised and supervised.

So what can you do once you've been matched with someone? There are countless activities you can do together: going on days out; baking cakes together (Vera's speciality); playing football in the park; helping with homework – basically, anything you might do with your own children or grandparents. In addition, we will be organising fun days from time to time so you can meet other people who are taking part in the scheme, swap notes and just have fun together.

So, why not give it a go? Pop into your local library or village hall to pick up a leaflet and application form, or ring us now on 0799 687 9313.

"Miss Havisham"

from *Great Expectations* by **Charles Dickens**

In this extract, Pip, who lives with his older sister, has been sent for by Miss Havisham: the mysterious and very rich lady who lives nearby. His uncle, Mr Pumblechook, has left him at the door and a young girl, Estella, is taking him into the house.

We went into the house by a side door – the great front entrance had two chains across it outside – and the first thing I noticed was, that the passages were all dark, and that she had left a candle burning there. She took it up, and we went through more passages and up a staircase, and still it was all dark, and only the candle lighted us.

At last we came to the door of a room, and she said, 'Go in.'

I answered, more in shyness than politeness, 'After you, miss.'

To this she returned: 'Don't be ridiculous, boy; I am not going in.' And scornfully walked away, and – what was worse – took the candle with her.

This was very uncomfortable, and I was half afraid. However, the only thing to be done being to knock at the door, I knocked, and was told from within to enter. I entered, therefore, and found myself in a pretty large room, well lighted with wax candles. No glimpse of daylight was to be seen in it. It was a dressing-room, as I supposed from the furniture, though much of it was of forms and uses then quite unknown to me. But prominent in it was a draped table with a gilded looking-glass, and that I made out at first sight to be a fine lady's dressing-table.

Whether I should have made out this object so soon if there had been no fine lady sitting at it, I cannot say. In an arm-chair, with an elbow resting on the table and her head leaning on that hand, sat the strangest lady I have ever seen, or shall ever see.

She was dressed in rich materials – satins, and lace, and silks – all of white. Her shoes were white. And she had a long white veil dependent from her hair, and she had bridal flowers in her hair, but her hair was white. Some bright jewels sparkled on her neck and on her hands, and some other jewels lay sparkling on the table. Dresses, less splendid than the dress she wore, and half-packed trunks, were scattered about. She had not quite finished dressing, for she had but one shoe on – the other was on the table near her hand – her veil was but half arranged, her watch and chain were not put on, and some lace for her bosom lay with those trinkets, and with her handkerchief, and gloves, and some flowers, and a prayer-book all confusedly heaped about the looking-glass.

It was not in the first few moments that I saw all these things, though I saw more of them in the first moments than might be supposed. But I saw that everything within my view which ought to be white, had been white long ago, and had lost its lustre and was faded and yellow. I saw that the bride within the bridal dress had withered like the dress, and like the flowers, and had no brightness left but the brightness of her sunken eyes. I saw that the dress had been put upon the rounded figure of a young woman, and that the figure upon which it now hung loose had shrunk to skin and bone. Once, I had been taken to see some ghastly waxwork at the fair, representing I know not what impossible personage lying in state. Once, I had been taken to one of our old marsh churches to see a skeleton in the ashes of a rich dress that had been dug out of a vault under the church pavement. Now, waxwork and skeleton seemed to have dark eyes that moved and looked at me. I should have cried out, if I could.

'Who is it?' said the lady at the table.

'Pip, ma'am.'

'Pip?'

'Mr. Pumblechook's boy, ma'am. Come – to play.'

'Come nearer; let me look at you. Come close.'

It was when I stood before her, avoiding her eyes, that I took note of the surrounding objects in detail, and saw that her watch had stopped at twenty minutes to nine, and that a clock in the room had stopped at twenty minutes to nine.

'Look at me,' said Miss Havisham. 'You are not afraid of a woman who has never seen the sun since you were born?'

I regret to state that I was not afraid of telling the enormous lie comprehended in the answer 'No.'

'Do you know what I touch here?' she said, laying her hands, one upon the other, on her left side.

'Yes, ma'am.' (It made me think of the young man.)

'What do I touch?'

'Your heart.'

'Broken!'

She uttered the word with an eager look, and with strong emphasis, and with a weird smile that had a kind of boast in it. Afterwards she kept her hands there for a little while, and slowly took them away as if they were heavy.

'I am tired,' said Miss Havisham. 'I want diversion, and I have done with men and women. Play.'

I think it will be conceded by my most disputatious reader, that she could hardly have directed an unfortunate boy to do anything in the wide world more difficult to be done under the circumstances.

'I sometimes have sick fancies,' she went on, 'and I have a sick fancy that I want to see some play. There, there!' with an impatient movement of the fingers of her right hand; 'play, play, play!'

Remembering Schooldays

Writing in 1871, Thomas Goodman, then an elderly man, remembers his schooldays at Oundle. The head teacher, Mr Bullen, is referred to as 'the master' and the other teachers as 'ushers'.

The cane was very generally used in the school. Indeed the ushers (of whom there were four) were allowed to use it, but the birch was reserved for special occasions only. I remember once, when Mr Bullen was caning a boy who seemed terribly frightened at the punishment, he exclaimed, "Oh pray, Sir, don't because you are in a passion," to which he replied by an interrogation, "Am I in a passion?" When the boy immediately answered, "Oh no, Sir, you are not in a passion," the master then rejoined, with a sharper cut of the cane than ever, "but I am in a passion."

Oundle had a very convenient river for bathing and occasionally, I believe more to save the trouble of feet-washing than anything else, we were taken down to the river, in one part of which those who were unable to swim might venture to bathe with safety. But when the art had been acquired, they were allowed to go into deeper water, and the elder Mr Dix sometimes, for fun's sake, used to take hold of a boy with one hand at the wrist, and another at the ankle, and throw him several yards into deep water – a feat which seemed to gratify the swimmer as an evidence of his skill and courage. I remember a boy once coming behind me when I was swimming and seizing me by the neck, sent me down several feet under the water, and I believe I am right in the assumption that my eyes were open, and able to see the fish as they swam along.

We had no other playground than the churchyard. There were many walnut trees planted in the churchyard; two of which, in the north-west corner, a retired spot, served capitally for a swing, which was also a favorite pastime with the boys, and many became skilful either at swinging themselves standing upon the rope, or, putting one leg above the rope and the other under it, turning themselves over repeatedly while they were at full swing. … There was considerable danger in boys jumping from one gravestone to another and sometimes in jumping over the tombstones. I was once attempting to go over one which was very easy on the one side but difficult on the other, as the slab at the top was far from being level… I caught my toe against the edge of the stone and my body went upon the ground with such violence that I began to think I should never get my breath again and I naturally abstained from making a second effort.

We were very irregular in our walks. Indeed, according to my recollections, we scarcely ever took them except on Sunday evenings, but I think we must have done so occasionally on other days, as I know it was a great treat to hear Mr Dix tell a story as we clustered round him at the river side, which he composed as he walked along with a pipe or cigar in his mouth – the smoking of which gave him time to recollect himself.

The punishments at Oundle School were very badly and unjustly regulated, in consequence of which the ushers were much more severe than the master, especially in their tasks. The latter would occasionally order a boy to write a sheet of paper, which, being foolscap, would of course, if properly filled, take up a considerable time, but the ushers would more frequently set half a dozen sheets. Again the amount depended upon what they were to write, the usual custom being to state the offence which had been committed as, for example, "I must not jump over the desks" or "I must get up when the bell rings". It often happened that a boy would get his companions to help him in writing these tasks, and it was thought to be done more expeditiously[1] if one boy wrote the letter "I" from the top to the bottom of the sheet and another undertook to write the next word "must" in the same way, and so on to the end, until the whole of the sheets were filled. This practice, of course, was discovered and in its place a boy was desired to fill his paper by copying from some book, which would take him twice as long, if not more.

---

[1]*expeditiously* – quickly

The classical usher, named Hinde, while a boy was repeating his lesson, if he found him defective,[2] was accustomed to make him stand by his side and, taking hold of one of his ears, used to give it a pull for every mistake he made. This, I think, was always done in the absence of the master, for I don't believe Mr Bullen would have allowed such a cruel mode of torturing a boy, as with all the master's gusts of passion, he had his periods of patience and forbearance, and I do not think that upon the whole he was disliked by the pupils.

[2]*defective* – inadequate, not good enough

Questions 1–5 are about the "Adopt a Granny" scheme (on page 76 of the reading material).

1. From the second paragraph, give two reasons why children might not see their own grandparents.

1 mark

_____

_____

_____

_____

2. How, according to the writer, would each of the following benefit from the "Adopt a Granny" scheme?

2 marks

Older people	
Parents	
Children	

3. What two reasons do Vera and Stan give for joining the scheme?

1 mark

_____

_____

_____

_____

_____

SUBTOTAL

4. How does the writer reassure readers that the "Adopt a Granny" scheme is safe and genuine?

_____

_____

_____

_____

_____

_____

_____

5. This text has more than one purpose. Tick the boxes to show which **three** of the following statements accurately describe the writer's purpose. If you tick more than three statements, you will receive no marks.

The writer wants to persuade people to join the "Adopt a Granny" scheme.	
The writer wants to persuade readers to visit the Puddington area.	
The writer is informing us about the "Adopt a Granny" scheme.	
The writer argues that children do not need grandparents.	
The writer argues that children's lives are improved by knowing older people.	

Questions 6–11 are about the 'Miss Havisham' extract from *Great Expectations* (pages 77–78 of the reading material).

6. Pick out two details from the first paragraph which make the house seem unwelcoming.

_____

_____

_____

7. How would you describe the girl's attitude to Pip? Use evidence from the text to back up your opinion.

_____

_____

_____

_____

8. Pip describes Miss Havisham as 'the strangest lady I have ever seen, or shall ever see'. Explain in your own words what is strange about her appearance.

_____

_____

_____

_____

9. **(a)** Of which two things does Miss Havisham remind Pip?

_____

_____

_____

1 mark

(b) What do these comparisons tell us about the effect her appearance has on Pip?

_____

_____

_____

2 marks

10. When Miss Havisham puts her hands on her heart, it makes Pip 'think of the young man'. Who do you think 'the young man' might be?

_____

_____

_____

_____

_____

2 marks

11. How does Dickens create an air of mystery about Miss Havisham?

Think about:
- Pip's role as the narrator and his character
- the way the house and Pip's entry into it are described
- the way Miss Havisham is described
- what Miss Havisham says and does.

Use evidence from the text to support your ideas.

5 marks

_____

_____

_____

_____

_____

_____

_____

_____

_____

_____

_____

_____

_____

_____

SUBTOTAL

Questions 12–16 are about *Remembering Schooldays* (pages 79–80 of the reading material).

12. What does the boy mean when he says that Mr Bullen is 'in a passion'?

_____

_____

1 mark

13. Why would a boy be pleased if Mr Dix picked him up and threw him into the deep water?

_____

_____

_____

1 mark

14. Give two games played by the boys in the churchyard:

_____

_____

1 mark

15. Which of the following statements reflect Thomas Goodman's feelings about his schooldays?

Tick **three** of the statements below. If you tick more than three statements, you will receive no marks.

2 marks

He hated everything about Oundle.	
He thinks punishments were inconsistent and sometimes cruel.	
On the whole, he respects Mr Bullen.	
He had some enjoyable times at Oundle.	
He thinks all the ushers were very caring.	
He never thinks about his schooldays.	

16. In this text, Goodman describes the discipline at his school. What do you think would be the reaction of modern readers to this? Explain as fully as you can.

3 marks

_____

_____

_____

_____

_____

_____

_____

SUBTOTAL

Set C

KEY STAGE 3

Shakespeare Test Paper

English

Romeo and Juliet, As You Like It and Macbeth

Shakespeare Test Paper

Romeo and Juliet, As You Like It and Macbeth

First name _____

Last name _____

Date _____

Instructions

In the following pages you will find three questions which assess your reading and understanding of Shakespeare. Each is on a different play:

Romeo and Juliet	page 89
As You Like It	page 94
Macbeth	page 99

- **Only** answer the question on the play you have studied.

- Read the question carefully.

- Write your answer on lined paper.

- You have **45 minutes** to complete the task.

- When you have completed the test, you can mark your answer using pages 115 and 120–122 of the Answers and Mark Scheme section of this book.

- Enter your mark below:

MAXIMUM MARK	18		ACTUAL MARK	

Romeo and Juliet

> **Romeo and Juliet**
>
> **Act 3, Scene 2, lines 36–96**
> **Act 3, Scene 5, lines 168–242**
>
> In the first extract, the nurse tells Juliet that Romeo has killed her cousin Tybalt and has been banished from Verona. In the second, after the secret marriage of Romeo and Juliet, Juliet's father tells her that he will force her to marry Paris.

What do we learn from these extracts about the relationship between Juliet and her nurse?

Support your ideas by referring to both of the extracts printed on the following pages.

Romeo and Juliet

Act 3, Scene 2, lines 36–96

In this extract, after Friar Lawrence has married them, Juliet is waiting for news of Romeo, not knowing that he has killed Tybalt and has been banished from Verona.

JULIET	Ay me! What news? Why dost thou wring thy hands?	
NURSE	Ah, well-a-day! He's dead, he's dead, he's dead!	
	We are undone, lady, we are undone!	
	Alack the day! He's gone, he's kill'd, he's dead!	
JULIET	Can heaven be so envious?	
NURSE	Romeo can,	40
	Though heaven cannot. O Romeo, Romeo,	
	Whoever would have thought it? Romeo!	
JULIET	What devil art thou, that dost torment me thus?	
	This torture should be roar'd in dismal hell.	
	Hath Romeo slain himself? Say thou but 'Ay,'	45
	And that bare vowel 'I' shall poison more	
	Than the death-darting eye of cockatrice:	
	I am not I, if there be such an 'Ay',	
	Or those eyes shut, that make thee answer 'Ay'.	
	If he be slain, say 'Ay'; or if not, 'No':	50
	Brief sounds determine of my weal or woe.	
NURSE	I saw the wound, I saw it with mine eyes –	
	God save the mark – here on his manly breast.	
	A piteous corse, a bloody piteous corse;	
	Pale, pale as ashes, all bedaub'd in blood –	55
	All in gore-blood; I swounded at the sight.	
JULIET	O, break, my heart! Poor bankrupt, break at once!	
	To prison, eyes, ne'er look on liberty!	
	Vile earth, to earth resign. End motion here;	
	And thou and Romeo press one heavy bier!	60
NURSE	O Tybalt, Tybalt, the best friend I had!	
	O courteous Tybalt! Honest gentleman!	
	That ever I should live to see thee dead!	
JULIET	What storm is this that blows so contrary?	
	Is Romeo slaughter'd, and is Tybalt dead?	65
	My dear-loved cousin, and my dearer lord?	

	Then, dreadful trumpet sound the general doom!	
	For who is living, if those two are gone?	
NURSE	Tybalt is gone and Romeo banished;	
	Romeo that kill'd him, he is banished.	70
JULIET	O God! Did Romeo's hand shed Tybalt's blood?	
NURSE	It did, it did. Alas the day, it did!	
JULIET	O serpent heart, hid with a flowering face!	
	Did ever dragon keep so fair a cave?	
	Beautiful tyrant! Fiend angelical!	75
	Dove-feather'd raven! Wolvish-ravening lamb!	
	Despised substance of divinest show!	
	Just opposite to what thou justly seem'st,	
	A damned saint, an honourable villain!	
	O nature, what hadst thou to do in hell,	80
	When thou didst bower the spirit of a fiend	
	In moral paradise of such sweet flesh?	
	Was ever book containing such vile matter	
	So fairly bound? O that deceit should dwell	
	In such a gorgeous palace!	
NURSE	There's no trust,	85
	No faith, no honesty in men; all perjured,	
	All forsworn, all naught, all dissemblers.	
	Ah, where's my man? Give me some aqua vitae:	
	These griefs, these woes, these sorrows make me old.	
	Shame come to Romeo!	
JULIET	Blister'd be thy tongue	90
	For such a wish! He was not born to shame:	
	Upon his brow shame is ashamed to sit;	
	For 'tis a throne where honour may be crown'd	
	Sole monarch of the universal earth.	
	O, what a beast was I to chide at him!	95
NURSE	Will you speak well of him that kill'd your cousin?	

Act 3, Scene 5, lines 168–242

In this extract, Juliet has just said goodbye to Romeo after their first night together. However, her father tells her that he will force her to marry Paris.

NURSE	God in heaven bless her!	
	You are to blame, my lord, to rate her so.	
CAPULET	And why, my lady wisdom? Hold your tongue,	170
	Good prudence. Smatter with your gossips, go.	
NURSE	I speak no treason.	
CAPULET	O, God 'I' good e'en.	
NURSE	May not one speak?	
CAPULET	Peace, you mumbling fool!	
	Utter your gravity o'er a gossip's bowl;	
	For here we need it not.	
LADY CAPULET	You are too hot.	175
CAPULET	God's bread! It makes me mad: day, night, work, play,	
	Alone, in company, still my care hath been	
	To have her match'd: and having now provided	
	A gentleman of noble parentage,	
	Of fair demesnes, youthful, and nobly lined,	180
	Stuff'd, as they say, with honourable parts,	
	Proportion'd as one's thought would wish a man;	
	And then to have a wretched puling fool,	
	A whining mammet, in her fortune's tender,	
	To answer 'I'll not wed; I cannot love,	185
	I am too young; I pray you, pardon me.'	
	But, as you will not wed, I'll pardon you.	
	Graze where you will you shall not house with me.	
	Look to't, think on't, I do not use to jest.	
	Thursday is near; lay hand on heart. Advise.	190
	And you be mine, I'll give you to my friend;	
	And you be not, hang, beg, starve, die streets,	
	For, by my soul, I'll ne'er acknowledge thee,	
	Nor what is mine shall never do thee good.	
	Trust to't, bethink you. I'll not be forsworn.	195
		Exit
JULIET	Is there no pity sitting in the clouds,	
	That sees into the bottom of my grief?	
	O, sweet my mother, cast me not away!	
	Delay this marriage for a month, a week;	
	Or, if you do not, make the bridal bed	200
	In that dim monument where Tybalt lies.	

| LADY CAPULET | Talk not to me, for I'll not speak a word: |
| | Do as thou wilt, for I have done with thee. |

Exit

JULIET	O God! O nurse, how shall this be prevented?	205
	My husband is on earth, my faith in heaven.	
	How shall that faith return again to earth,	
	Unless that husband send it me from heaven	
	By leaving earth? Comfort me, counsel me.	
	Alack, alack, that heaven should practise stratagems	
	Upon so soft a subject as myself!	210
	What say'st thou? Hast thou not a word of joy?	
	Some comfort, nurse.	

NURSE	Faith, here it is.
	Romeo is banish'd; and all the world to nothing,
	That he dares ne'er come back to challenge you;
	Or, if he do, it needs must be by stealth.	215
	Then, since the case so stands as now it doth,
	I think it best you married with the county.
	O, he's a lovely gentleman!
	Romeo's a dishclout to him: an eagle, madam,
	Hath not so green, so quick, so fair an eye	220
	As Paris hath. Beshrew my very heart,
	I think you are happy in this second match,
	For it excels your first: or if it did not,
	Your first is dead; or 'twere as good he were,
	As living here and you no use of him.	225

| JULIET | Speakest thou from thy heart? |

| NURSE | And from my soul too; |
| | Or else beshrew them both. |

| JULIET | Amen! |

| NURSE | What? |

JULIET	Well, thou hast comforted me marvellous much.	230
	Go in: and tell my lady I am gone,
	Having displeased my father, to Laurence's cell,
	To make confession and to be absolved.

| NURSE | Marry, I will; and this is wisely done. |

Exit

JULIET	Ancient damnation! O most wicked fiend!	235
	Is it more sin to wish me thus forsworn,
	Or to dispraise my lord with that same tongue
	Which she hath praised him with above compare
	So many thousand times? Go, counsellor!
	Thou and my bosom henceforth shall be twain.	240
	I'll to the friar, to know his remedy:
	If all else fail, myself have power to die.

Exit

As You Like It

As You Like It

Act 1, Scene 1, lines 26–82
Act 2, Scene 3, lines 1–77

In the first extract, Orlando confronts his brother, Oliver, about the way he has treated him since their father's death. In the second, Adam warns him not to return home as his life is in danger.

What impressions might an audience get of Orlando from these extracts?

Support your ideas by referring to both of the extracts printed on the following pages.

As You Like It

Act 1, Scene 1, lines 26–82

In this extract, Orlando argues with his brother, Oliver, about the way he has been treated since their father's death.

ADAM	Yonder comes my master, your brother.	
ORLANDO	Go apart, Adam, and thou shalt hear how he will shake me up.	
	Enter OLIVER	
OLIVER	Now, sir! What make you here?	
ORLANDO	Nothing. I am not taught to make anything.	30
OLIVER	What mar you then, sir?	
ORLANDO	Marry, sir, I am helping you to mar that which God made, a poor unworthy brother of yours, with idleness.	
OLIVER	Marry, sir, be better employed, and be naught awhile.	
ORLANDO	Shall I keep your hogs and eat husks with them? What prodigal portion have I spent, that I should come to such penury?	35
OLIVER	Know you where you are, sir?	
ORLANDO	O, sir, very well; here in your orchard.	
OLIVER	Know you before whom, sir?	40
ORLANDO	Ay, better than him I am before knows me. I know you are my eldest brother; and, in the gentle condition of blood, you should so know me. The courtesy of nations allows you my better, in that you are the first-born; but the same tradition takes not away my blood, were there twenty brothers betwixt us. I have as much of my father in me as you; albeit, I confess, your coming before me is nearer to his reverence.	45
OLIVER	What, boy! (*strikes him*)	50
ORLANDO	Come, come, elder brother, you are too young in this. (*seizes him*)	
OLIVER	Wilt thou lay hands on me, villain?	

	This I must do, or know not what to do.	35
	Yet this I will not do, do how I can.	
	I rather will subject me to the malice	
	Of a diverted blood and bloody brother.	
ADAM	But do not so. I have five hundred crowns,	
	The thrifty hire I saved under your father,	40
	Which I did store to be my foster-nurse	
	When service should in my old limbs lie lame	
	And unregarded age in corners thrown.	
	Take that, and He that doth the ravens feed,	
	Yea, providently caters for the sparrow,	45
	Be comfort to my age! Here is the gold.	
	And all this I give you. Let me be your servant.	
	Though I look old, yet I am strong and lusty;	
	For in my youth I never did apply	
	Hot and rebellious liquors in my blood,	50
	Nor did not with unbashful forehead woo	
	The means of weakness and debility.	
	Therefore my age is as a lusty winter,	
	Frosty, but kindly. Let me go with you.	
	I'll do the service of a younger man	55
	In all your business and necessities.	
ORLANDO	O good old man, how well in thee appears	
	The constant service of the antique world,	
	When service sweat for duty, not for meed!	
	Thou art not for the fashion of these times,	60
	Where none will sweat but for promotion,	
	And having that, do choke their service up	
	Even with the having. It is not so with thee.	
	But, poor old man, thou prunest a rotten tree	
	That cannot so much as a blossom yield	65
	In lieu of all thy pains and husbandry.	
	But come thy ways. We'll go along together,	
	And ere we have thy youthful wages spent,	
	We'll light upon some settled low content.	
ADAM	Master, go on, and I will follow thee	70
	To the last gasp, with truth and loyalty.	
	From seventeen years till now almost fourscore	
	Here lived I, but now live here no more.	
	At seventeen years many their fortunes seek,	
	But at fourscore it is too late a week.	75
	Yet fortune cannot recompense me better	
	Than to die well, and not my master's debtor.	

Exeunt

Macbeth

Macbeth

Act 1, Scene 7, lines 28 to the end
Act 5, Scene 1, lines 18–61

In the first extract, Lady Macbeth persuades her husband to go through with the murder of Duncan. In the second, she is seen walking and talking in her sleep.

What do we learn about the character of Lady Macbeth from these extracts?

Support your ideas by referring to both of the extracts printed on the following pages.

Macbeth

Act 1, Scene 7, lines 28 to the end

In this extract, Lady Macbeth tries to persuade Macbeth to kill King Duncan.

Enter LADY MACBETH

MACBETH	How now? What news?
LADY MACBETH	He has almost supped. Why have you left the chamber?
MACBETH	Has he asked for me?
LADY MACBETH	Know you not he has?

MACBETH We will proceed no further in this business.
He hath honoured me of late, and I have bought
Golden opinions from all sorts of people,
Which would be worn now in their newest gloss,
Not cast aside so soon.

LADY MACBETH Was the hope drunk
Wherein you dressed yourself? Hath it slept since?
And wakes it now to look so green and pale
At what it did so freely? From this time,
Such I account thy love. Art thou afeard
To be the same in thine own act and valour,
As thou art in desire? Wouldst thou have that
Which thou esteem'st the ornament of life,
And live a coward in thine own esteem,
Letting I dare not wait upon I would,
Like the poor cat i'th'adage?

MACBETH Prithee, peace.
I dare do all that may become a man.
Who dares do more is none.

LADY MACBETH What beast was't then
That made you break this enterprise to me?
When you durst do it, then you were a man.
And to be more then what you were, you would
Be so much more the man. Nor time, nor place
Did then adhere, and yet you would make both.
They have made themselves and that their fitness now
Does unmake you. I have given suck and know
How tender 'tis to love the babe that milks me:
I would, while it was smiling in my face,
Have plucked my nipple from his boneless gums
And dashed the brains out, had I so sworn
As you have done to this.

30

35

40

45

50

55

MACBETH	If we should fail?
LADY MACBETH	We fail!

But screw your courage to the sticking place 60
And we'll not fail. When Duncan is asleep,
Whereto the rather shall his day's hard journey
Soundly invite him, his two chamberlains
Will I with wine and wassail so convince
That memory, the warder of the brain, 65
Shall be a fume, and the receipt of reason
A limbeck only. When in swinish sleep
Their drenched natures lie as in death,
What cannot you and I perform upon
Th'unguarded Duncan? What not put upon 70
His spongy officers, who shall bear the guilt
Of our great quell?

MACBETH   Bring forth men-children only,
For thy undaunted mettle should compose
Nothing but males. Will it not be received,
When we have marked with blood those sleepy two 75
Of his own chamber and used their very daggers,
That they have done't?

LADY MACBETH   Who dares receive it other,
As we shall make our griefs and clamour roar
Upon his death?

MACBETH   I am settled and bend up
Each corporal agent to this terrible feat. 80
Away, and mock the time with fairest show,
False face must hide what the false heart doth know.

Exeunt

Act 5, Scene 1, lines 18–61

In this extract, the doctor and Lady Macbeth's gentlewoman watch her as she sleep walks.

Enter LADY MACBETH *with a taper*

GENTLEWOMAN	Lo you, here she comes. This is her very guise, and,	
	Upon my life, fast asleep. Observe her. Stand close.	
DOCTOR	How came she by that light?	20
GENTLEWOMAN	Why, it stood by her. She has light by her continually.	
	'Tis her command.	
DOCTOR	You see her eyes are open.	
GENTLEWOMAN	Ay, but their sense is shut.	
DOCTOR	What is it she does now? Look how she rubs her hands.	25
GENTLEWOMAN	It is an accustomed action with her, to	
	seem thus washing her hands; I have known her	
	to continue in this a quarter of an hour.	
LADY MACBETH	Yet here's a spot.	
DOCTOR	Hark, she speaks. I will set down what comes	30
	from her to satisfy my remembrance the more strongly.	
LADY MACBETH	Out damned spot! Out, I say! One, two. Why then 'tis	
	time to do't. Hell is murky. Fie, my lord, fie, a soldier,	
	and afeard? What need we fear? Who knows it, when none	
	can call our power to account? Yet who would have thought	35
	the old man to have had so much blood in him?	
DOCTOR	Do you mark that?	

LADY MACBETH	The Thane of Fife had a wife. Where is she now? What, will these hands ne'er be clean? No more o'that, my lord, no more o'that. You mar all this with starting.	40
DOCTOR	Go to, go to; you have known what you should not.	
GENTLEWOMAN	She has spoke what she should not, I am sure of that. Heaven knows what she has known.	
LADY MACBETH	Here's the smell of blood still. All the perfumes of Arabia will not sweeten this little hand. O, O, O!	45
DOCTOR	What a sigh is there? The heart is sorely charged.	
GENTLEWOMAN	I would not have such a heart in my bosom for the dignity of the whole body.	
DOCTOR	Well, well, well –	50
GENTLEWOMAN	Pray God it be, sir.	
DOCTOR	This disease is beyond my practice. Yet I have known those which have walked in their sleep who have died holily in their beds.	
LADY MACBETH	Wash your hands, put on your nightgown, look not so pale. I tell you again, Banquo's buried. He cannot come out on's grave.	55
DOCTOR	Even so?	
LADY MACBETH	To bed, to bed; there's knocking at the gate. Come, come, come, come, give me your hand. What's done cannot be undone. To bed, to bed, to bed.	60

Exit

Set
C

KEY STAGE 3

Writing Test
Paper

English

Making an Impression

Writing Test Paper

Making an Impression

First name _____

Last name _____

Date _____

Instructions

- There are two writing tasks in this paper.

- The test is **1 hour and 15 minutes** long.

- You should spend: **45 minutes** on Section A (the longer writing task)
  30 minutes on Section B (the shorter writing task).

- You may spend the first 15 minutes planning your answer to Section A. Your plan will not be marked.

- Section A has 30 marks.

- Section B has 20 marks.

- Write your answer on lined paper.

- When you have finished, check your work carefully.

When you have completed the test, you can mark your answer using pages 123–128 of the Answers and Mark Scheme section of this book.

- Enter your marks below:

	Mark	Maximum mark
Section A		30
Section B		20
Total		50

Section A

Longer Writing Task

If I could meet . . .

A television programme has launched a competition for young people, asking them to write an essay about a person they look up to but have never met. The winners will get the opportunity to present a programme about their heroes.

Here is the competition brief:

We all have people we look up to in our lives – heroes or role models. Some of them are people close to us; but others are well-known people we have never met, perhaps even figures from history.

We want you to write about the person you would most like to meet. It can be anyone well-known (alive or dead) – a writer, a musician, a politician, an actor – anyone you find inspiring.

You should include:
- some background information about the person
- the reasons you find him/her inspirational
- the influence he/she has had on you and other people
- anything you would to ask him/her if you did meet.

Write your essay.

Section B

Shorter Writing Task

Thanks for the present

Your grandmother is having a long holiday with some other relatives in Australia. She missed your birthday but sent you a present. She does not like using computers so you have decided to write a letter, thanking her for the present and telling her your news.

Here's the note enclosed with her present:

> Sorry I couldn't be there for your birthday. I hope you had a wonderful time.
>
> I'm enclosing a little something for you – hope the colour suits and I got your size right!
>
> I've decided to stay on here with Joe, Marlene and the children for another month. I'm having a great time but missing you all.
>
> I'd love to hear all about what you've been up to while I've been gone.

Write your letter.

Answers and Mark Scheme

The following pages include answers and mark schemes for all the practice papers.

Use them to mark your papers and when you have arrived at a total mark for each test, keep a note of them to use them to keep track of your progress as you complete all three sets.

Reading Test Answers

Set A – 'Into the Woods!'

'The Way Through the Woods'

1. They have shut/closed the road through the woods.   *(1 mark for **both** answers. 0 marks for one only)*
    They have planted trees.

2. **(a)** anemone   *(1 mark for **all 3** correct)*
    (b) ring-dove
    (c) badger

3. Give yourself a mark for any of the following up to maximum of two: *(Maximum 2 marks)*
    *   He is the only person who still goes into the woods.
    *   He knows the woods better than anyone else does.
    *   Because of his job, he knows a lot about nature and the woods.

4. Give yourself a mark for any **one** of the following: *(1 mark)*
    *   It makes the reader pause and think about what has gone before.
    *   It makes you wonder what has been left out.
    *   It tells you that the poet has something else to say.

5. Look at the statements below and give yourself the number of marks (maximum 5) for the one which most closely describes your answer.

    You have made one or two simple points about the language and content of the passage, e.g. *Nobody goes in the woods* or *You can hear strange things in the woods.*   *(1 mark)*

    You have shown that you are aware of how the language helps to create the atmosphere, answering at least two bullet points, e.g. pointing out how it is described as being very quiet because nobody goes there before something is heard, or commenting on repetition.   *(2 marks)*

    You have shown that you understand how the language and content create an impression of mystery and the supernatural. You have answered all three bullet points briefly, quoting from the text. You might have commented on the focus on nature taking over the path, on the description of natural sounds, and on the effects of repetition.   *(3 marks)*

You have explored how the language and content create the atmosphere. You have answered all three bullet points, supporting your points with quotations. You might have commented on the peaceful atmosphere created in the first stanza, the way the poet chooses to describe sounds rather than sights in the second stanza, and the slight changes to the repeated phrase about the way through the woods. *(4 marks)*

Your answer is full and focused, addressing all three bullet points fully and using short quotations to back up your points effectively. You have shown a high level of awareness of the writer's techniques (e.g. use of refrain; onomatopoeia) and their effect on the reader. You might have included a personal response. *(5 marks)*

'Westerly Woods Adventure Park '

6. '…covered in a blanket of deep snow'. *(1 mark)*

7. They might prefer to have company/be with other people. *(1 mark for **both** answers. 0 for one)*
    They might like the help/guidance of a guide/expert.

8.

People being appealed to	Phrase from the text
People who feel they need a good rest	*Comfortable and stress-free*
People who like to meet new people on holiday	*A whole village*
People who like to feel they're close to nature	*Clustered round the tranquil natural lake which lies at the centre of the woods* (either *'clustered round the tranquil natural lake'* or *'at the centre of the woods'* would be enough)

(1 mark for two correct answers. 2 marks for three correct answers – maximum 2)

9. Give yourself 1 mark for each of the following (or similar) points: *(Maximum 2 marks)*
    *   They accommodate large numbers and young people often like to stay together.
    *   As the facilities are described as 'basic' they are probably quite cheap so young people could afford to stay there.

10. Look at the statements below and give yourself the number of marks (maximum 3) for the one which most closely describes your answer.

    You have made one or two simple points. You might have picked out one word or phrase, e.g. *'thrill-seekers' sounds like they want people who like excitement.* *(1 mark)*

    You have picked out at least two phrases, explaining them, and mentioning both 'fun' and 'excitement', e.g. *the writer gives examples of activities a lot of people find fun, like climbing ropes or going down slides and the use of the word 'challenge' suggests it might not be easy and so is more exciting.* *(2 marks)*

    Your answer is focused. You have picked out at least three phrases, explaining them and relating them to the idea that the trails are exciting and fun. You might have mentioned all the examples given above and perhaps 'with a difference' or 'physical and mental skills through fun'. *(3 marks)*

'The Wild Wood' from *The Wind in the Willows*

11. 'with great cheerfulness of spirit' *(1 mark)*

12. Give yourself a mark for any **two** of the following: *(1 mark. 0 marks if only one given)*
- 'logs tripped him'
- 'trees crowded nearer and nearer'
- 'holes made ugly mouths'

13. The answers below are suggestions. Give yourself a mark for any other reasonable interpretation (but not paraphrasing of the quotations).

And then – yes! – no! – yes!	Mole is not sure whether the faces are real or not. At the end he thinks they are.
Certainly a little narrow face, with hard eyes, had flashed up	He is sure that he has really seen something and it was not attractive.
...all fixing on him with evil glances of malice and hatred	He now sees so many of them that he knows he cannot be mistaken. He is also sure that they are dangerous/evil.

(1 mark for two correct answers, 2 marks for three)

14. (a) The use of the phrase 'at first' suggests that Mole will soon realise that his first thought was wrong. Give yourself a mark for any similar answer – but the phrase 'at first' must be mentioned. *(1 mark)*

(b) Give yourself a mark for any of the following: *(1 mark)*
- another animal, which might attack mole;
- the animals with the evil faces;
- whatever was hiding in the woods;
- a human being;
- something evil and dangerous.

15.

Mole imagines the faces.	False
The faces and noises are all made by the rabbit.	False
At the end of the extract we do not know whose faces they are.	True
At the end of the extract Mole is safe.	False
At the end of the extract the rabbit is safe.	True

(1 mark if three or four answers are correct. 2 marks if all answers are correct)

16. Look at the statements below and give yourself the number of marks (maximum 5) for the one which most closely describes your answer.

You have made one or two simple points about the language and content of the passage, e.g. *The mole is scared* or *There are strange things in the woods*. *(1 mark)*

You have shown that you are aware of how the language helps create the atmosphere, answering at least two bullet points, e.g. pointing out that Mole starts off happy and confident in spite of not knowing the woods, or saying that lots of little things happen to make him more frightened. *(2 marks)*

You have shown that you understand how the language and content create an impression of mystery and the supernatural. You have answered at least three bullet points briefly, quoting from the text. You might have commented on the short sentences ending in 'began' and the way Mole's mood changes as he realises he is not imagining things. *(3 marks)*

You have explored how the language and content create the atmosphere. You have answered all four bullet points, supporting your points with quotations. You might have commented on the way Mole's cheerfulness contrasts with the descriptions of the woods, the way the darkness closes in and the mystery of what is making the faces and noises. *(4 marks)*

Your answer is full and focused, addressing all three bullet points fully and using short quotations to back up your points effectively. You have shown a high level of awareness of the writer's techniques (e.g. the way in which we see it from Mole's point of view; the imagery of the forest; the contrast between the small vulnerable animal and the huge unknown woods) and their effect on the reader. You might have shown a personal response. *(5 marks)*

Reading Test Answers

Set B – 'Catching the Train'

'The Railways of Victorian Britain.'

1. A train (at least one train) had to stop at each station every day.
    Trains had to include third class carriages. *(1 mark for **both** answers. 0 marks if only one given)*

2. He booked trains from all over the country and charged people a fixed price to include return travel and entrance to the Great Exhibition. *(1 mark for part of the above. 2 marks for all of the above)*

3.

The Football league was founded	5
The Railway act was passed	1
The first FA cup final was held	4
Bank holidays were introduced	3
King's Cross station was opened	2

(All answers must be correct – 1 mark)

4. Give yourself a mark for any two of the following (or similar) answers, up to a maximum of two marks:
    *   They show how many different activities/the variety of activities the Victorians could enjoy because of the railways.
    *   They illustrate some of the things mentioned so we can get a better idea of what it was like.
    *   They are icons that we can click to lead us to more information. *(Maximum 2 marks)*

5. Give yourself a mark for any of the following points, up to a maximum of three:
   - They allowed people to travel greater distances.
   - They made travel more affordable/cheaper so that poorer people could travel.
   - They gave people the opportunity to go to new places and events.
   - They helped to make sporting events more popular.
   - They helped to create the idea of the 'day trip' or excursion. *(Maximum of 3)*

'Saviours of the Train' from *The Railway Children*

6. A rustling, whispering sound. *(1 mark)*

7. 'as though it were a living creature and were walking down the side of the cutting'; 'bringing up the rear like some old shepherd…' *(1 mark for each – maximum 2 marks)*

8. He knows when the train is due (11.29).
   He knows how fast it goes (there is not enough time to get to the station).
   He knows that cutting the telegraph wires would not help.
   (1 mark for two of these points; 2 marks for all three points)

9. **(a)** The station is too far away and they would not get there in time. *(1 mark)*
   (b) They could only cut the wires, which would not help/they would not be able to get up there (give yourself a mark for either of these). *(1 mark)*
   (c) As they often wave to the trains, nobody would take any notice. *(1 mark)*

10. Look at the answers below to see which is closest to yours and give yourself the appropriate number of marks:
    - If the children wave something the driver is more likely to notice them: they usually just wave their hands. *(1 mark)*
    - The petticoats are red and would attract attention because of their colour. *(2 marks)*
    - Red is associated with/symbolises danger and so the driver would realise it was a warning/the train was in danger. *(3 marks)*

11. Look at the statements below and give yourself the number of marks (maximum 5) for the one which most closely describes your answer.

    You have made one or two simple points about the children in general or just one of the children, e.g. *The children are brave* or *Peter knows a lot about the trains.* *(1 mark)*

    You have shown that you are aware of the children's characters, answering at least two bullet points, e.g. mentioning that they are confused at first and a bit frightened but soon try to find a solution to the problem, or noticing that Phyllis is the most frightened of the three. *(2 marks)*

    You have shown that you understand how the language and content create an impression of the children's characters. You have answered all three bullet points briefly or two in greater detail, quoting from the text. You have mentioned all three of the children, distinguishing between their characters. *(3 marks)*

    You have explored aspects of all three characters as well as how they get on and act together. You have answered all three bullet points in some detail, supporting your points with quotations. You might have commented on the different ways the excitement and fear affects them. You might have mentioned how each one takes a different role (Bobbie being the oldest, Peter the boy and Phyllis the youngest) as well as how they discuss the situation and come up with a solution together. *(4 marks)*

Your answer is full and focused, addressing all three bullet points and using short quotations to back up your points effectively. You have shown a high level of awareness of the writer's techniques and their effect on the reader. You might have commented on the use of dialogue and the way they speak to each other and/or the contrast between their wonder at the 'magical' happenings and their practical common sense when they realise what is actually happening. You might have given a personal response. A good answer could deal with each bullet point in turn or write about each child in turn before commenting on them as a group.

(5 marks)

'Beijing to Shanghai Railway'

12. '...like a flying saucer has just landed from outer space.' *(1 mark)*

13. He says that it is so clean he can see the guard's reflection in the polished granite. *(1 mark)*

14. It must be a very smooth ride/it is not a rough or bumpy journey. *(1 mark)*

15.

The article is about a train journey.	
Each section starts with a time.	✓
The writer describes what he sees.	
There is a lot of information in the article.	
The article is written in the present tense.	✓

*(1 mark for **both** correct answers. 0 marks if more than two boxes ticked.)*

16. Give yourself a mark for any of the following (or similar) answers, up to a maximum of 3 marks:
   - He writes a lot about how modern the train is before mentioning more traditional aspects of Chinese life.
   - He says how quickly the train goes past the people working in the fields.
   - He looks out and sees people still working the same way they have done for centuries, with very little technology, while he is on a very advanced train.
   - He mentions the tombs of people's ancestors in the fields, which reminds us of how things have been the same for centuries (until now).
   - He notices how different the north and south are, and always have been, yet they are now connected by the high speed train.

(Maximum 3 marks)

Reading Test Answers

Set C Answers – 'Young and Old'

'Adopt a Granny'

1. Their grandparents could be dead.
    They might live a long way away (in this country or abroad). *(1 mark for **both**)*

2.

Older people	Contact with young people makes them feel younger.
Parents	They could get help with, and advice about, bringing up children.
Children	Older people have more time to play with them and listen to them.

(1 mark for two correct answers; 2 marks for three)

3. They were missing their own grandchildren.
    They were bored/finding life a bit boring. *(1 mark for **both**)*

4. Give yourself a mark for any of the following answers, up to maximum of 3 marks:
    - S/he mentions that it is a registered charity.
    - S/he says they work closely with the local authority.
    - S/he mentions that checks have to be made before people can join.
    - S/he says that everything they do is properly organised and supervised. *(Maximum 3 marks)*

5.

The writer wants to persuade people to join the "Adopt a Granny" scheme.	✓
The writer wants to persuade readers to visit the Puddington area.	
The writer is informing us about the "Adopt a Granny" scheme.	✓
The writer argues that children do not need grandparents.	
The writer argues that children's lives are improved by knowing older people.	✓

(1 mark for two correct, 2 for three – 0 marks if more than three boxes ticked)

'Miss Havisham'

6. There are two chains across the entrance.
    The passages are all dark. *(1 mark for **both** answers)*

7. Give yourself a mark for any of the following:
    Points: She looks down on him/she is unfriendly/she appears to be snobbish or distant.
    Evidence: She tells him what to do ('go on')/she addresses him as 'boy'/she is described as walking away
    'scornfully.' *(1 mark for the point and one mark for supporting quotation – maximum of 2 marks)*

8. Give yourself a mark for any of the following (or similar) answers, up to a maximum of 2 marks:
    - She is dressed as a bride and her clothes and jewels are very expensive, but the clothes are faded and yellowish.
    - She is old and thin, so the clothes do not fit her.
    - It seems very strange for such an old woman to be dressed as a bride. *(Maximum 2 marks)*

9. **(a)** A waxwork (of someone lying in state) at the fair.
  A skeleton (dug up from the vaults of the church). *(1 mark for **both**)*

   (b) Give yourself a mark for any of the following (or similar) answers, up to a maximum of 2 marks:
   - She seems to him to be more dead than alive/like a dead person or thing come to life.
   - She is a bit frightening but at the same time fascinating.
   - He finds her appearance unpleasant/repulsive but has to look at her.
   - He is shocked/horrified by what he sees.
   - He does not really think of her as a living person. *(Maximum 2 marks)*

10. Look at the answers below, decide which is closest to your answer, and give yourself the appropriate mark:
   It is a young man from her past who let her down. *(1 mark)*
   It is a young man who promised to marry her and then left her/died (on her wedding day). *(2 marks)*

11. Look at the statements below and give yourself the number of marks (maximum 5) for the one which most closely describes your answer.

   You have made one or two simple/ general points, e.g. *Pip thinks she is very strange* or *It is dark in the house*. *(1 mark)*

   You have shown some awareness of the atmosphere created, addressing at least two bullet points, e.g. mentioning that Pip is brought to the house not knowing what to expect, or that the house is described as if no-one lives there. *(2 marks)*

   You have shown that you understand how the language and content create an air of mystery. You have answered at least three bullet points briefly or two in greater detail, quoting from the text. You might have mentioned how the reader only sees what Pip sees or that we are made to wonder what the explanation is for Miss Havisham's odd appearance. *(3 marks)*

   You have answered all three bullet points in some detail and have supported your points with quotations. You might have commented on how nothing is explained to Pip before he meets her, the gloomy atmosphere, the almost ghost-like appearance of Miss Havisham and the oddness of her request at the end of the extract. *(4 marks)*

   Your answer is full and focused, addressing all four bullet points and using short quotations to back up points effectively. You have shown a high level of awareness of the writer's techniques and their effect on the reader. You might have commented on the language used to describe both the room and Miss Havisham, the way the different characters speak and the comparisons Pip makes. You might have given a personal response. *(5 marks)*

'Remembering Schooldays'

12. He was in a bad temper/he was angry. *(1 mark)*

13. It showed that he considered them good enough swimmers to go in the deep water. *(1 mark)*

14. Swinging on a rope.
   Jumping over tombstones. *(1 mark for both)*

15.

He hated everything about Oundle.	
He thinks punishments were inconsistent and sometimes cruel.	✓
On the whole, he respected Mr Bullen.	✓
He had some enjoyable times at Oundle.	✓
He thinks all the ushers were very caring.	
He never thinks about his schooldays.	

(1 mark for two correct answers, 2 marks for three. 0 marks if more than four boxes ticked)

16. Any of the following (or similar) points:
- They would be shocked/horrified/outraged.
- They would be surprised *or* they would not be surprised because they knew how different it was.
- They would think that it was wrong.
- They would think it was very different from now.
- They would find it funny/be amused because of the way Goodman describes it.
- They would be glad it is not like that now.
- They would not understand why people put up with it.   *(1 mark for each valid point up to maximum of 3)*

Shakespeare Test Answers

When you are marking your Shakespeare answer, first decide which description your answer most closely resembles. Then give it a mark depending on whether it matches 1, 2 or 3 of the statements given.

Mark Scheme

1–3 marks
- You have given a few simple facts and opinions about the extracts.
- There may be some misunderstanding/answers may not always be relevant.
- You have retold the 'story' of the extracts or copied out sections of it.

4–6 marks
- You have given a little explanation, showing some awareness of the needs of the question.
- Your comments are relevant but mostly about the plot.
- You have made some broad references to how the characters speak.

7–9 marks
- You have shown some general understanding of the question, although some points might not be developed.
- You have made some comments on the language the characters use.
- Some of your points are backed up with reference to the text.

10–12 marks
- You have discussed how the extracts relate to the question, even though all the ideas might not be of equal quality.
- You have shown awareness of the characters' use of language and its effects.
- Most of your points are backed up with reference to the text.

13–15 marks

- There is a clear focus on how the extracts relate to the question.
- You have made good, consistent comments on the characters' language and its effect on the audience.
- You have chosen quotations well and linked them together to present an overall argument.

16–18 marks

- You have analysed every quotation in depth in relation to the question and there is evaluation.
- You have commented on every quotation in terms of the language that the characters use.
- You have picked out individual words from quotations and linked them into the overall argument.

Shakespeare Tests: Examples of Possible Content

On the following pages, you will find examples of the kind of comments pupils might make when answering each of the questions in the practice papers.

They do not represent 'correct' answers or points that you must make, but they will help you to relate the mark scheme to the particular question you have answered.

Some of these suggested comments cover only one extract; others focus on a few lines. You will be expected to cover **both extracts** in detail in order to gain good marks. Your answers, especially those gaining higher marks will, of course, be much longer. They should be written in complete sentences with points developed and connected.

Shakespeare Tests – Set A

Romeo and Juliet

1–3 marks

Juliet is in love with Romeo and cannot wait to see him. Juliet does not want Romeo to leave.

4–6 marks

Juliet's feelings are confused because she loves Romeo but he has killed her cousin. Juliet pretends to Romeo that it is still night so that he will not leave her.

7–9 marks

The strength of her love is shown by her emotional reaction to the nurse's news and by the risks she takes. In the first extract she wants it to be night but in the second she wants it to be day ('it is the nightingale and not the lark').

10–12 marks

The audience might be a bit confused by her reactions in the first extract and might think they show how young she is. A lot of her language relates to death and makes us feel she has no hope ('dreadful trumpet sound the general doom').

13–15 marks

Juliet's opening soliloquy establishes her mood. She uses imagery to express her impatience: 'gallop apace, you fiery footed steeds'. Her mood changes when the nurse enters. Convinced that Romeo is dead, she thinks of her own death: 'and thou and Romeo press one heavy bier'. At the start of the second extract she wants the moment to last for ever but, even though she is in love, she dwells on death: 'I have an ill–divining soul!'

16–18 marks

In her opening soliloquy, Juliet expresses the strength of her feelings and her desire for Romeo to the audience. She longs for 'love–performing night' to help her consummate her love. These scenes both take place in the dark, reflecting the secret and forbidden nature of her love. In the second extract she wants Romeo to stay, because she loves him, and to go, because he is in danger. Her deliberate confusion of the lark and the nightingale reflects this dilemma. She ends with a terrible premonition of Romeo 'dead in the bottom of a tomb', as he will be at the end of the play.

As You Like It

1–3 marks

Orlando and his brother do not get on. Adam, Orlando's servant, goes to the forest with him.

4–6 marks

Orlando fights with his older brother, who treats him like a servant. They do not act as brothers should. Adam shows more loyalty to Orlando and offers to help him escape to the forest.

7–9 marks

Orlando tells the story of how he has been treated by his brother – like the 'animals on his dunghill.' He picks a quarrel with Oliver, who calls him 'boy' and 'villain'. There is no brotherly love between them. Adam shows he is on Orlando's side by saying he will follow him and help him. This shows love and loyalty.

10–12 marks

Orlando's speech is about a lack of family love. Oliver has not treated Orlando as a brother should: 'his horses are bred better'. Orlando provokes Oliver so we can see what he is really like. Adam tries to make them behave like brothers but Oliver turns on him. He has served the family loyally but is called an 'old dog'. Orlando, on the other hand, says Adam shows 'the constant service of the antique world', suggesting that this is how people should behave but things have changed for the worse.

13–15 marks

Orlando's first speech introduces the theme of family love and loyalty, and of families breaking up. He is angry with his brother for treating him like 'his animals on the dunghill'. This image reminds us of the story of the prodigal son and Orlando asks 'what prodigal portion have I spent', implying that, unlike the prodigal son, he has done nothing to deserve ill–treatment. Oliver's cruelty is contrasted with the love and loyalty of Adam, who is willing to serve and help Orlando 'to the last gasp.'

16–18 marks

Orlando tells Oliver that 'in the gentle condition of blood, you should know me.' This means that he is Oliver's equal in birth. It also reflects the idea that brothers should look after each other and that what Oliver is doing is unnatural. Oliver also treats Adam as an 'old dog'. While Orlando deserves better treatment because of his 'blood', Adam deserves it because of his 'service'. The values 'of the antique world' are being destroyed by Oliver, as they are by Duke Frederick, who has also turned against his brother.

Macbeth

1–3 marks

Macbeth murders Duncan but is not sure and says he is afraid. At the end he is worried about the battle.

4–6 marks

Macbeth has killed Duncan but is worried about all the noises and something saying 'sleep no more' but Lady Macbeth tells him not to be stupid. He is brave when he is preparing for the battle and is ready to die.

7–9 marks

Macbeth seems nervous, asking questions and talking about noises. He is worried about not being able to say 'amen'. This is because he has done such an evil deed. He is full of guilt. At the end he is in a different mood and seems not to care about anything, even Lady Macbeth's death because he says 'she should have died hereafter'. He is angry with the messenger but knows the prophecies are coming true. This seems to make him determined and brave.

10–12 marks

At first Macbeth and Lady Macbeth speak in short sentences because it is very tense and they are nervous. When he describes what is worrying him she does not seem to understand: 'a foolish thing to say a sorry sight'. Hearing someone say 'Macbeth does murder sleep' is a sign of his guilty conscience. He changes as the play goes on and in the second scene he says, 'I have almost forgot the taste of fears'. Now he is brave and reckless.

13–15 marks

Because Macbeth has committed such a terrible sin he will 'sleep no more.' He feels he cannot ever get rid of the guilt. His mood is different in the second extract and he says Lady Macbeth 'should have died hereafter.' Perhaps he is saying she died too young or perhaps that she would have died anyway. He is philosophical and resigned to his fate: 'Life's but a walking shadow'. He knows the prophecies are coming true. This seems to make him determined and brave.

16–18 marks

At the beginning Macbeth is nervous and worried, shown by his choppy speech and questions. Lady Macbeth does not understand, telling him to 'consider it not so deeply'. But Macbeth's guilt is overwhelming. He keeps repeating that 'I could not say Amen'. This is important because it is as if he is cut off from God, so he cannot pray. Sleep is also very significant in the play. It is 'innocent' and he is guilty so he will 'sleep no more.' In the second extract he reflects on life, which he sees as 'full of sound and fury, signifying nothing' but at the end he is defiant and impressive as he vows to 'die with harness on our back.'

Shakespeare Tests – Set B

Romeo and Juliet

1–3 marks

Romeo is in love with a girl who does not love him. He stays behind after the party to tell Juliet he loves her.

4–6 marks

In the first scene Romeo thinks he loves Rosaline and talks all about love. After that he falls in love with Juliet. This is true love and in the balcony scene they tell each other how much they are in love.

7–9 marks

Romeo has been acting oddly and he tells his cousin that he is love. He talks a lot about love and how it does not make sense: 'feather of lead, bright smoke'. He seems to enjoy being miserable. In the second extract he looks up to Juliet, who is on her balcony, and compares her to the sun. He uses a lot of language about the sun, the stars and the moon to show how great his love is.

10–12 marks

Romeo talks in the first scene all about love rather than about the girl he loves, using oxymoron, e.g. 'cold fire' and 'sick health' to express how it makes him feel. She will never have him because she has sworn to 'live chaste'. His love is pointless. In contrast, when he falls in love with Juliet she falls in love with him. In the second extract she is placed above him and his language ('bright angel') suggests he almost worships her. We know she returns his love because she talks about it in a soliloquy, which she does not know he can hear.

13–15 marks

In the first extract Romeo is 'playing with words', trying to express the contradictions of love, 'a madness most discreet'. The fact that his love will never be returned seems to add to its attraction. The second extract shows how his love for Juliet is returned equally. Romeo uses a series of images to describe Juliet: the moon is 'envious' of her and her beauty would 'shame those stars'. Juliet returns his feelings, as she shows in her speech, so this love is quite different but it is doomed in another way.

16–18 marks

In the first scene Romeo might be playing a part – the part of the 'melancholy lover' – which would be familiar to Shakespeare's audience. He enjoys 'the fume of sighs' as well as the 'fire sparkling in a lover's eyes' and his language is clever and entertaining. The fact that Rosaline will never return his love only adds to his enjoyment. When he falls in love with Juliet so quickly we might think it is the same again – so in the second scene he has to convince us as well as her of his sincerity.

As You Like It

1–3 marks

Rosalind falls in love with Orlando at the wrestling match. The shepherd is in love with Phoebe.

4–6 marks

At the wrestling match, Rosalind falls in love with Orlando because he was a friend of her father, the old Duke. We also see how she and her cousin Celia love each other in spite of their fathers. When she hears Silvius talking about Phoebe, she sympathises.

7–9 marks

After Orlando wins the wrestling match, Rosalind gives him a chain to wear for her. It is not clear whether she has fallen in love with him. Silvius's love is not returned he does not believe anyone can love like him ('thou hast not loved') and Rosalind feels sorry for him as she is also in love ('this shepherd's passion/is much upon my fashion').

10–12 marks

After Orlando reveals his identity, Rosalind recalls that her father loved his father 'as his soul'. Her father has been overthrown by the new Duke, Frederick, who says, 'I wouldst thou hadst been son to some man else'. In spite of this Rosalind loves his daughter, Celia. She gives Orlando a token, showing she is falling in love with him. She goes to the forest not knowing whether he loves her. Her love might be unrequited like Silvius's love for Phoebe: 'Alas, poor shepherd! Searching of thy wound, I have by hard adventure found mine own,'

13–15 marks

As Rosalind and Celia watch the wrestling match, they seem amused, excited and attracted to him, Rosalind crying out 'O excellent young man!' When she finds out who his father is, and that her father loved his 'as his soul,' it makes her love him, just as it makes Frederick hate him. She does not openly say she loves him but drops hints ('overthrown more than your enemies') and the giving of the chain is a symbolic gesture. In the second extract we see an exaggerated portrayal of unrequited love in Silvius, whose speeches, spoken in verse with a repeated 'thou hast not loved', might seem funny.

16–18 marks

The wrestling match brings family relationships into focus: Rosalind and Celia are close in spite of their fathers' enmity and Orlando is effectively fighting his brother. Rosalind seems to fall in love with Orlando almost because of his father's loyalty to hers – as if love can be inherited. Silvius is a figure out of the pastoral tradition – a romantic idea of a shepherd – almost a parody, with his miserable verse and the refrain of 'thou hadst not loved'. Touchstone responds with a crude tale of being in love with Jane Smile, showing us another extreme of love, but Rosalind empathises, seeing his love as 'mush upon my fashion.'

Macbeth

1–3 marks

Macbeth tells the murderers to kill Banquo. He is scared when he sees the ghost.

4–6 marks

Macbeth has to persuade the murderers to kill Banquo. He tells them he was their enemy. He is pleased that he will get rid of Banquo. When he sees the ghost no-one else sees it so he has to act terrified and as if he really believes he sees it.

7–9 marks

Macbeth is now the king and he needs to show that he is strong and confident. He goes on about how Banquo is their enemy and how low they are: 'in the catalogue ye go for men' making them think they will be manlier if they kill Banquo. At the end of the scene he should be happy because he has got what he wants. At the start of the second extract he has seen the ghost and is recovering. He should be a bit scared but trying to hide it from the guests.

10–12 marks

Macbeth should seem sincere because he is relying on the murderers. Even though he is the king he has to flatter them a bit. When they agree he says 'your spirits shine through you' so he must be very pleased and relieved, smiling and maybe shaking their hands. When he has seen the ghost he moves away from the table and tries to put a brave face on, toasting 'our dear friend Banquo' but when the ghost comes back his fear shows as he shouts out 'Avaunt! And quit my sight!

13–15 marks

In the first extract his speech is calm and confident. He should be aware that he is the king now and in command, confidently lying to the murderers ('Know that it was…') and asking them long questions to get a reaction (Do you find…?' Are you so gospell'd…?'). His speeches should seem rehearsed as this is all planned. By contrast, the ghost of Banquo is totally unexpected and he has to show real fear and horror, jumping up, shouting 'Avaunt!' He reacts to Lady Macbeth by saying he is as brave as any man but this makes him show fear, his mood frightening everyone else.

16–18 marks

Macbeth is the only person who can see Banquo's ghost. Whether he is looking at another actor or an empty space he has to convince the audience that he really sees it and express his horror and his guilt. At the start of the extract he makes a huge effort to be calm and says he has 'a strange infirmity'. He could say this slowly as if he is thinking hard of an excuse and calming himself. When he toasts Banquo ('Would he were here!') his gestures might be a bit too big and his voice too loud.

Shakespeare Tests – Set C

Romeo and Juliet

1–3 marks

Juliet is upset because of Romeo and Tybalt. The nurse looks after Juliet.

4–6 marks

Juliet is upset because she thinks the nurse is telling her that Romeo is dead but it is Tybalt who is dead. The nurse has brought her up and has been her best friend but she takes her father's side.

7–9 marks

Juliet is confused by what the nurse tells her and turns on her, calling her a 'devil'. When Juliet attacks Romeo, the nurse agrees with her but this makes Juliet attack the nurse ('blister'd be thy tongue'). In the second extract the nurse at first supports Juliet but later tells her to marry Paris. Juliet realises she now has no-one to turn to but the Friar.

10–12 marks

The nurse has been Juliet's close confidante and Juliet relies on her to help her and to take messages so she only knows what the nurse tells her and when the nurse cries 'he's dead!' she thinks it is Romeo. When she realises it is Tybalt who is dead she is angry and impatient with the nurse. Juliet's emotions change so quickly in this scene the nurse cannot keep up. Although she knows Juliet loves Romeo she still asks: 'Will you speak well of him that kill'd your cousin?'

13–15 marks

In the second extract, Juliet's relationship with the nurse changes completely. At first, the nurse steps in to defend her, bravely standing up to Capulet: 'You are to blame, my lord, to rate her so.' This shows her closeness to Juliet and would make the audience think that she will try to help Juliet. However, when Juliet's parents leave she seems to take their side. According to her, Romeo is 'dead: or ''twere as good he were'. She seems to want to help Juliet but not to understand her feelings.

The first extract shows a comic misunderstanding as the nurse, in vivid, melodramatic language ('a piteous corse, a bloody piteous corse'), gives the news of Tybalt's death and Juliet thinks she is talking about Romeo. This lack of understanding becomes more serious in the next extract as the pragmatic nurse, choosing to ignore the couple's marriage, tells Juliet to treat the 'dishclout' Romeo as if he were dead and marry Paris. Juliet's reaction is cool and controlled as she fools the nurse into thinking she agrees, telling her with heavy irony, 'thou hast comforted me marvellous much'.

As You Like It

1–3 marks

Orlando is a good character. His brother wants to kill him so he goes to the forest.

4–6 marks

Orlando has been badly treated by his brother and treated as a servant so he is angry and wants his rights. He does not want to run away but Adam persuades him and he shows that he appreciates Adam.

7–9 marks

Orlando stands up to Oliver and confronts him with the bad treatment he has received. He is in the right and does not deserve to be called 'villain'. He deserves better because of 'the gentle condition of blood'. Adam respects Orlando and wants to help him, so he thinks he is a good man. Orlando also respects Adam, who is a good servant.

10–12 marks

Orlando's speech about his treatment gains the audience's sympathy. Oliver has not treated Orlando as a brother should and Orlando ironically calls himself 'a poor unworthy brother'. He provokes Oliver so Adam (and the audience) can see what he is really like. Orlando is quite aggressive and tries to 'lay hands' on Oliver. He is also proud and insulted by being called 'villain'. Adam shows that he believes in Orlando by offering to help him and Orlando returns his love and respect, saying that Adam shows 'the constant service of the antique world'.

13–15 marks

Orlando is angry with his brother for treating him badly since their father's death. He refers to the story of the prodigal son, asking if he should 'keep your hogs', as the son in the story did, but, unlike the prodigal son he has done nothing wrong and has had no 'prodigal portion' to waste. The audience might see him as proud – and aggressive when he physically attacks his brother – but they are likely to sympathise with his position, especially when Oliver threatens to have him killed. Oliver's cruelty is contrasted with the love and loyalty of Adam, who is willing to serve and help Orlando 'to the last gasp.'

16–18 marks

Orlando tells Oliver that 'in the gentle condition of blood, you should know me.' This means that he is Oliver's equal in birth. This might give some people the impression he is too keen on his status as a nobleman but most would think he has been unjustly deprived of his rights. It also reflects the idea that brothers should look after each other and that what Oliver is doing is unnatural. The values 'of the antique world' are being destroyed by Oliver, as they are by Duke Frederick, who has also turned against his brother.

Macbeth

1–3 marks

Macbeth is worried about murdering Duncan but Lady Macbeth tells him he has to. Then she goes mad and sleep walks.

4–6 marks

Lady Macbeth is a lot stronger than Macbeth. He thinks it is wrong to kill the king but she says he is a coward and she will help him. In the second extract she has changed and keeps washing her hands, showing she has a guilty conscience.

7–9 marks

Lady Macbeth is annoyed with Macbeth when he says 'we will proceed no further in this business.' This means he does not want to kill Duncan. She says if he does not do it he will be a 'coward'. She says some very shocking things, even that she would kill her own child rather than not kill Duncan. This shows her cruelty and her determination. In the sleep-walking scene she is very different. She relives the murder of Duncan and wants to get rid of the guilt: 'Out damned spot'.

10–12 marks

In the first extract Lady Macbeth shows how strong and ruthless she is. Although it was Macbeth who first thought of the murder, she is at least as ambitious and she bullies him into doing it, saying she will not love him if he does not do it ('Such I account thy love' and questioning his manhood 'When you durst do it, then you were a man.') She has no sense of right and wrong and shows this in the horrible image of dashing out her baby's brains. Macbeth seems to love and admire her for this, telling her to 'bring forth men-children only.'

13–15 marks

In contrast with the ambitious, determined woman who thought her husband a coward because he had a conscience, in the second extract Lady Macbeth finally shows some weakness. Trying to wash out the 'damned spot' reminds us of how earlier she said a little water would clear them of the deed. Now she says 'Hell is murky' as if she feels she will go there and, like Macbeth did after the murder, she now cannot see how she can get rid of the guilt: 'All the perfumes of Arabia will not sweeten this little hand.'

16–18 marks

Lady Macbeth's questions and her mocking tone seem designed to provoke a reaction from Macbeth. His reply ('…who dares do more is none') sounds like it should be the last word, but she turns it against him, shockingly suggesting that the murder of an old man in his sleep is a 'manly' thing to do. She seems to want to prove she is more of a man than he is but her idea of what makes a man in perverse and grotesque. She says she knows 'how tender 'tis to love the babe', perhaps making the audience momentarily see a softer, 'womanly' side to her, but then she chillingly describes how she would dash out its brains.

Writing Test Answers

The two writing tests are marked for different elements of writing and each attracts a different number of marks. Make sure you use the right mark scheme for the task you are marking.

When you look at the mark schemes you will see that different descriptions have different numbers of marks for them.

When you are marking your writing test answers, decide which description your answer most closely resembles. Give it a mark according to how closely it matches the statements given.

Longer Writing Task: Mark Scheme

This mark scheme applies to the Longer Writing Tasks in Sets A, B and C. There are three parts to the mark scheme. The first two ('Sentence Structure and Punctuation' and 'Text structure and Organisation') are exactly the same for all three practice papers. The third section ('Composition and Effect') includes guidance on how you might gain marks in each of the practice papers.

The total number of marks available is 30.

Sentence Structure and Punctuation

0 marks
- You may have used some simple connectives, such as 'and' and 'but', but sentences are usually simple.
- You have used some full stops, capital letters, question marks and exclamation marks.

1–2 marks
- You have used connectives such as 'if' and 'because', and the relative pronouns 'who' and 'which' to form some complex sentences.
- You have used full stops, question marks and exclamation marks accurately. You have used commas in sentences, usually correctly, and speech marks if needed.

3–4 marks
- You have used a wide range of connectives to make clear relationships between ideas, e.g. 'although', 'meanwhile' or 'on the other hand'. Your sentences vary in length and structure.
- You have used a variety of punctuation, mostly accurately, e.g. commas to mark subordinate clauses and correct punctuation of speech, if needed.

5–6 marks
- You have used a variety of sentence structures to create effect, e.g. starting sentences with subordinate clauses ('After a short period, they…' 'Despite her feelings, she…') or using short sentences. You might have used modal verbs such as 'could' or 'may'.
- You have used a range of punctuation, e.g. brackets for asides, commas to mark subordinate clause, semi-colons and colons – with few errors.

7 marks

- You have varied your sentence lengths to create interesting effects, with appropriate connectives used. You have used a range of sentences structures and techniques to create effects, e.g. repetition, contrast, fragments. The passive voice might be used, e.g. 'it was thought that…'
- You have used a full range of punctuation accurately and skilfully to assist the meaning and create a pleasing effect.

8 marks

- You have used a wide range of sentence types with skill and accuracy to clarify meaning and interest the reader. There might be some unusual or creative use of sentence structure.
- You have used a full range of punctuation correctly, adding to the effect of the writing.

Text Structure and Organisation

0 marks

- You have made some attempt to organise writing, putting connected ideas together.
- You might have used paragraphs, but without much logic.

1–2 marks

- You have used paragraphs starting with the main topic.
- The piece has a recognisable beginning and end.

3–4 marks

- You have used paragraphs of different lengths, arranged in a logical order.
- There are a clear introduction and conclusion.

5–6 marks

- You have arranged detailed content well within and between paragraphs.
- Your paragraphs are connected, using phrases such as 'on the other hand' and 'as a result of this'.

7 marks

- Your paragraphs are varied in length to suit the content. They are linked with a range of appropriate words and phrases.
- Your paragraphs are arranged in a controlled way to interest the reader, e.g. flashbacks in a narrative or argument and counter-argument.

8 marks

- You have organised and shaped your writing in a controlled way, designed to involve the reader.
- You have used paragraphing or other organisational devices imaginatively.

Composition and Effect

0 marks

- You have a general idea of the purpose and audience.
- There is some relevant content.
  Practice Paper A – You have given some information about the park and an opinion.
  Practice Paper B – You have written about the railway and have given one or two arguments.
  Practice Paper C – You have written about a person and have given a reason for your choice.

1–3 marks

- Your purpose is clear.
- You try to interest the reader.
- You have developed some ideas in detail.

Practice Paper A – You have given more detailed information. You have mentioned both positive and negative aspects, e.g. that there is plenty to do but it is very expensive.

Practice Paper B – You show understanding of the problem. You have reported arguments on both sides e.g. it will spoil the views but it might bring business to the area.

Practice Paper C – You have explained reasons for your choice. You have tried to make the person sound interesting to the reader.

4–6 marks

- Your writing engages the reader's interest.
- You have explored a range of relevant ideas in some detail.
- Your viewpoint is clear.

Practice Paper A – You have given a range of information. You have considered negative and positive aspects and have made clear judgement, e.g. that, on balance, you would recommend it for families with young children but not for older people.

Practice Paper B – You have set out arguments for and against in more detail and have ended with some thoughtful proposals, e.g. that the council look more closely at the compensation available to people who might suffer because of the railway.

Practice Paper C – You have written convincingly about the qualities of the person described and conveyed your enthusiasm for her/him, e.g. saying that s/he has shown bravery and determination in achieving their fame.

7–9 marks

- You have used a range of techniques to achieve your purpose.
- You have taken into account the reader's viewpoint.
- Your view is well-argued and consistent.

Practice Paper A – Your writing is entertaining as well as informative. You arrive at a convincing conclusion, e.g. that although you did not enjoy many aspects of the experience, your children had a great time and want to return, so you would recommend that parents give it a try.

Practice Paper B – Your writing has an impersonal tone. You have given several arguments for and against, a succinct summary of the debate and some clear proposals/ideas e.g. that your meeting felt that the government had not set out a convincing case for the new railway and you would like the council to come up with alternatives.

Practice Paper C – You have given a detailed and enthusiastic description of the chosen person. You have written convincingly about what makes him/her a good role model, and have included interesting/entertaining ideas about the meeting, e.g. saying that the qualities s/he has shown in their career have inspired you to aim higher and that if you met them, you would ask them what advice s/he would give to their younger self.

10–12 marks

- Your style is well-judged, using a wide range of techniques.
- Your tone is appropriate for both purpose and audience.
- All the content is relevant and used to support the argument.

Practice Paper A – You have given a sense of your personality and viewpoint with enough detailed information to allow the reader to form an opinion, e.g. describing various attractions, reporting the views of different groups of people and giving clear information about pricing, accessibility etc.

Practice Paper B – Your writing reads like an official report. You have summarised a range of arguments and have offered well-judged proposals and ideas e.g. giving brief accounts of all the arguments put, and who put them, grouping similar ideas together and making a judgment about the feelings of the majority.

Practice Paper C – Your writing is imaginative and creative, putting forward convincing arguments and successfully engaging the reader, e.g. giving some amusing anecdotes about your subject (and maybe about yourself) and saying what this tells you about them or coming up with some questions for them which are different from those usually asked of celebrities.

13–14 marks

- You have shown complete understanding and control of purpose and audience.
- There is a strong individual style, created by the use of a range of techniques.
  Practice Paper A – You have written a sophisticated and creative review. It does everything asked for above but from an original, individual viewpoint.
  Practice Paper B – Your report is thorough and balanced, and is professionally presented. It does everything asked for above but from an original, individual viewpoint.
  Practice Paper C – Your writing is original, entertaining and possibly moving. It does everything asked for above but from an original, individual viewpoint.

Shorter Writing Task: Mark Scheme

This mark scheme applies to the Shorter Writing Tasks in Sets A, B and C. There are three part to the mark scheme. The first two ('Spelling' and 'Sentence Structure, Punctuation and Paragraphing') are exactly the same for all three practice papers. The third part ('Composition and Effect') includes guidance on how the bullet points might be achieved in each of the practice papers.

The total number of marks available is 20.

Spelling

0 marks

- You have spelt simple (mostly one syllable) words correctly.
  Down/grass/young/chair/eat/pencil/finger

1 mark

- You have spelt simple words, including more common words with more than one syllable, correctly, e.g. adverbs ending in 'ly', verbs ending in 'ed' and 'ing', and most plurals.
  Crowded/ smiling/ sincerely/slowly/reason/honest/donkeys/flies/women

2 marks

- You have spelt more complex words that fit regular patterns correctly, e.g. words with prefixes such as 'dis', 'un' or 'pre'; suffixes such as 'tion' or 'ful'; common homophones.
  Beautiful/disappoint/unnatural/knowledge/frequently/education/whose/whether

3 marks

- Most spelling, including that of irregular words, is correct.
  Initials/mischievous/vicious/principle/efficient/seize/aggressive/definitely

4 marks

- Almost all spelling, including that of complex irregular words, is correct.
  Colossal/precocious/accommodation/occasionally/occurred/chronological

Sentence Structure, Punctuation and Paragraphing

0 marks

- You use simple sentences; you might use linking words such as 'and' and 'but'. You have used full stops and capital letters.
- You might have used paragraphs.

1–2 marks

- You have used sentences of different lengths. You have used a variety of connectives, including relative pronouns. You have used commas, full stops and question marks, usually correctly.
- You have used paragraphs, mainly in a logical order, containing some detail.

3–4 marks

- You have used a variety of sentence lengths and types, and a range of connectives. You have correctly used a range of punctuation, including commas for subordination. If needed, you have correctly used punctuation for speech.
- You have developed your ideas within paragraphs, which are linked to achieve a logical whole.

5 marks

- Your sentences are varied in length and type to achieve appropriate effects. You have used a wide range of punctuation – brackets, dashes, colons and semicolons – usually correctly.
- You have used paragraphs of different lengths, appropriate to their content, within a well-structured piece. Your ideas are developed in an interesting way within them.

6 marks

- You have used a wide range of sentence structures to achieve particular effects. You have used a wide range of punctuation correctly to make meaning clear.
- Your paragraphs are linked effectively to create a pleasing whole. The ideas within them are linked and developed in a sophisticated way.

Composition and Effect

0 marks

- You have a general idea of the purpose and audience.
- There is some relevant content.
  Practice Paper A – Your writing looks like a letter. In it, you apply for a job.
  Practice Paper B – You have given some information about an attraction.
  Practice paper C – Your writing looks like a letter. In it, you say 'thank you'.

1–3 marks

- Your purpose is clear.
- You have tried to interest the reader.
- Your ideas are developed in detail.
  Practice Paper A – You have clearly written a letter, with the proper opening and closing. You have given relevant information, e.g. about your qualifications. You have attempted a formal tone.
  Practice Paper B – You have set out your writing like a leaflet, perhaps using headlines and bullet points. You have given relevant, positive information, e.g. describing all the things you can do at a leisure park.
  Practice Paper C – You have clearly written a letter, using an informal tone. You have given news and have shown an interest in the reader, e.g. telling her about your school trip and asking if she's planning any trips in Australia.

4–6 marks

- Your writing engages the reader's interest.
- The tone of your writing is consistent.
- Your viewpoint is clear.
  Practice Paper A – You have used an appropriate formal tone. You have expressed enthusiasm and have given interesting information, perhaps picking out details from your experience and saying why they would make you good at the job.
  Practice Paper B – You have given a range of information, e.g. about cinemas, leisure parks and places to eat. You have used a persuasive tone. Your writing is clearly aimed at young people.
  Practice Paper C – You have written an entertaining, chatty letter, clearly intended for an older family member, e.g. by focusing on things that have happened locally that might interest her and by not using text language etc.

7–9 marks

- You have used a range of techniques to achieve your purpose.
- Your tone is appropriate for both purpose and audience.
- Your view is well-argued and consistent.

  Practice Paper A – You have addressed all the requirements of the advertisement, 'selling' yourself convincingly, e.g. by saying how you have demonstrated various qualities in the past and how these would be useful in the future. You have written your letter in the correct form.

  Practice Paper B – You have addressed all the requirements of the competition in an entertaining, persuasive and creative way, e.g. organising the information in an attractive way, using quotations from happy visitors or giving a personal, quirky reaction to the place.

  Practice Paper C – You have given a detailed and enthusiastic account of your news, perhaps telling funny stories about what your family has been up to. You have engaged with the interests and concerns of the older recipient, e.g. discussing what's happening on her favourite TV programmes. You have used an appropriate form for an informal letter.

10 marks

- You show complete understanding and control of purpose and audience. There is a strong individual style, created by the use of a range of techniques.

  Practice Paper A – You have written a mature and convincing letter of application. It reads like the real thing.

  Practice Paper B – You have written an original, informative, persuasive and creative leaflet. Anyone reading it would want to visit your area.

  Practice Paper C – You have written an original, entertaining and possibly moving letter. Your own grandmother would love to receive it.